WAR CHILD

GROWING UP IN
ADOLF HITLER'S GERMANY

Tank,
I wish you peace!
Annelee Woodstrom

By Annelee Woodstrom

WAR CHILD
GROWING UP IN ADOLF HITLER'S GERMANY

Author - Annelee Woodstrom
Publisher - McCleery & Sons Publishing
German Photographs - Courtesy of *Nürnberger Erinnerungen 5*

International Standard Book Number: 1-931916-20-9
Printed in the United States of America

Dedicated to the legions of innocent men, women and children

of all nations drawn into wars.

Their suffering was often much greater than what

my family and I had endured.

THANK YOU

I wish that my parents and my husband, Kenny, were still living so I could thank them for the love and guidance they gave me. I want to thank the following people for their invaluable assistance: My own family for encouraging me to write. Francis Gibson who diligently worked with me until my sporadic writing became a book. My professional mentors, Paul Gruchow; and Cathy McMullen, who voiced their support at workshops and in articles they wrote about my endeavor. Kaye Hilde, Heidi Gizzo, Janet Skretvedt, and Marce Bentley who at times proofread, asked questions and made suggestions.

I tried to be truthful and correct in stating when and where events took place. The essays I wrote and the letters of my Papa, and the documents of the court proceedings against Anna Siller are still in my possession.

As a child, and during my adolescene, constant propaganda and strictly enforced censorship influenced my thinking. As a young adult, the bombings and all the consequential suffering caused by World War II affected me deeply. I like to think that through aging and passing of time, I have learned to be open minded and look at both sides of an issue before judgment or action.

I changed the names of several people or left them nameless to protect their identity.

My wish for my readers is that soon we may live <u>in</u> and <u>with</u> world peace and that everyone can enjoy and use each day God has given us.

WAR

Good-bye, my son, farewell.
It was just yesterday that I too went so you could
safely live and play.
Was it futile, in vain, what can I say?
The tiger is waiting for game we are told –
he threatens from afar.
Or is it just a mouse that is bold?
Does it matter what it is or who we are?
God's speed my son it matters much that you come
back to build a land we fought to keep us such
without division, hatred or guilt.
FAR AWAY – IN ANOTHER LAND –
where other people dwell,
A father says, "GOOD-BYE MY SON,
FAREWELL."

Annelee Woodstrom - February 1968

TABLE OF CONTENTS

CHAPTER ONE

INDOCTRINATION

Mitterteich, Bavaria, April 30, 1935. I was sure tomorrow was going to be the best "Day of National Labor" celebration ever because so far, this had been the most exciting week I had ever had in fourth grade.

On Monday, Sister Gabrielle told us, "Girls, if you keep up with your reading, there won't be any other assignments for this week."

All fifty-four of us looked unbelievingly at each other and wondered, "Was Sister Gabrielle sick? Worse yet, had she lost her mind?"

Sister Gabrielle couldn't bear the thought of being idle. She always gave homework, and even during vacation, she assigned just one more project.

Her favorite saying was, "Girls, always remember, 'Idle hands create nothing, they just make mischief while work creates and makes an eager mind.'"

Several hands shot up. We needed to make sure we had heard her correctly, but Sister Gabrielle didn't acknowledge our raised hands because to her, wasting time was a sin.

"I repeat, complete your reading. Since there won't be any other assignments for the remainder of the week, we will use some school time and your recess to make signs for the May Day parade. Herr Burgomaster Kegler asked for these slogans:

"One for All, and All for one!"

"Strength through Joy!"

"Work for the 1000 Year Reich!"

"You will work in groups of five or six." She went to the blackboard and explained, "Here are some examples of patterns you may copy." Quickly, with expertise, she drew several emblem designs while she went on: "Those of you who belong to the Hitler Maiden group must bring your signs to the market square on Friday after school. A Hitler Youth leader will put you to work and you will string garlands, cut grass, or collect flowers for the parade. If you march in Sunday's parade, you must be at the assigned starting point at 1:30 p.m. Uniforms must be pressed and your shoes must be shined."

All week long, Sister Gabrielle kept her word about no assignments. Now, it was Friday afternoon, and she gave us final instructions for the weekend.

"Girls, remember, you must always mind your parents. I expect that everyone will attend Mass on Saturday and Children's Service on Sunday."

She raised her long, slim hands. We rose, stood rigidly, and waited. "Now let us end the week with our usual hymn, 'Jesus I Live for You' and then we will close with the Lord's Prayer."

We watched for her cue and sang,

"Jesus, I live for you,
Jesus, I die for you.
Jesus, I am yours
while I live and when I die."

"Very good. Now bow your heads, close your eyes, and in this moment of silence, look inward, inward."

Slowly she led us in prayer. Before the last phrase of the "Holy Mary" prayer ended, most girls had left their inward station and concentrated on their school bags instead. Finally she dismissed us, row by row.

On our way home, Bertl, Inge, Mary, Karola, and I stopped here and there and watched as workers placed a speaker's podium at the market square. Several Hitler Youth leaders drew circles and squares on streets so each group could find its starting point while others stationed horse-drawn wagons loaded with freshly cut grass near the parade routes.

"Oh, I wish I were older!" Mary whined, "Then I could get a new Young Maiden's uniform like my sister Rosa has."

"You're so lucky," Bertl interrupted , "your mama and papa let Rosa join the Young Maidens. I bet when you are ten you can join, too."

"My cousins, Erna and Lisl, asked if they could join the League of German Maidens when they are fourteen," I said, "but Uncle Pepp and Uncle Franz said, 'No'! I know what Papa will say, 'Absolutely not, Anneliese, and that will be that.' You just wait, I will not give up. When I'm ten I still will ask him."

"I have to go home," Bertl reminded us. "Let's meet by Boderbauer's butcher shop after dinner. My mama said that we will see the best parade ever!"

Sauntering home, I watched while people swept sidewalks, washed windows, and decorated their homes. Mr. Engleman, the neighborhood handyman, fastened garlands to Mama's wooden flower boxes and he and Mama worked long into the evening, so everything would be ready when Papa came home.

The two most important men in my life were Uncle Pepp and Max, my Papa. Uncle Pepp, Papa's older brother, was so proud of being the first-born of the ten other siblings, and in his own opinion, he was the most successful man in our clan. He was six feet tall, slim as a rod, and he always walked straight like the Kaiser. Since his auburn hair was thinning, he parted in on the left side and combed the front-hair back from his forehead so that the crop-eared cut emphasized his high cheekbones. His deep-set, steel-blue eyes were less penetrating when they were shaded by the visors of his felt hat. The Roman nose, his thin lips, and the finely chiseled chin gave him the tall and stately appearance of a true Bavarian.

Uncle Pepp usually wore a snowy-white short-sleeved shirt neatly tucked into a pair of black leather knickerbockers all held in place by his favorite well-worn suspenders. A loden-gray jacket usually covered his long arms and bony wrists. His Bavarian socks and his black leather oxfords, which were shined to a high gloss for special occasions, completed his outfit. However, when he worked alongside his bakers, he wore the same white baker's pants, shirt and aprons as his crew. When he worked his fields, he would tell his wife, Aunt Nanni, "Any old thing will do when I work with the earth and its bounty."

Uncle Pepp's agility and sound judgment set him apart as a

man to be reckoned with, and it placed him in a position of authority not only with his family but townspeople as well.

Then there was Max, my Papa. He was the exact opposite of Uncle Pepp in stature and manner. He barely rose above Uncle Pepp's shoulders, and his sisters and brothers always teased Papa about being the Bavarian with red hair. He, too, had steel-blue eyes, the chiseled nose and chin, but he was stockier than Uncle Pepp. I didn't like it when his sisters called him their baby brother, but as long as no one else did, Papa didn't seem to mind. When Papa smiled at Mama, his blue eyes smiled, too. Then Mama would say, "Max, now don't you give me that look." I knew that Mama always would give in to what Papa wanted.

Even though Papa was most often working in other regions and towns, when he was home, he, too, commanded respect where ever he went. People who knew him well called him "Max", others removed their hats and said, "God's blessings, Mr. Max." But those who just knew that Papa lived in town addressed him as "Mr. Solch."

I was proud to be a part of this family and I was happy because tonight, Papa would come home for the May Day celebration.

"You returned our Fatherland to us."

CHAPTER TWO

MAY DAY CELEBRATION

May Day arrived. When Papa gave me spending money and told me that after church I could watch the parade with my friends, I knew nothing could spoil this perfect day. On our way to the High Mass, Papa and I watched as shiny cars of dignitaries blocked sidewalks, and horse-drawn carriages of visitors filled the sideways of every alley. Grandmas and parents checked their children's costumes or uniforms, and gave final instructions while the children listened restlessly, anxious to get out on their own. Marchers and spectators who had walked in from the surrounding towns milled about the market square and searched for a resting place.

As soon as the High Mass was over, I hurried outside. There was so much to see. A thick carpet of grass clippings hid the streets, small silver birches cut to size and fastened to the outside of houses covered the brick and stucco walls, and student banners held taut by wires hung high above the streets.

The life-size posters that covered the entryways to houses and barns caught my attention. One poster showed a young German worker dressed in a white, short-sleeve shirt and brown pants. The linen cloth tied around his neck was full of seeds. He held a fist full of kernels that he sprinkled over the slogan, "Work, Freedom, and Bread." His blond hair, blue eyes, forceful stance, and determined expression left no doubt that he was of Aryan descent. On another poster, a laborer rested his sinewy arms on three bricks that displayed the same slogan. The standards had varied designs in colors of red, white, and black, but each decoration blended in with the sea of fluttering swastika flags that hung from the windows of every attic. Miniature flags framed the lower windows and doors of homes.

The outdoor beer gardens were filled with farmers in their

native costumes. Some were engrossed in heated discussions with visitors and townspeople, others sat and pondered their next move in cards, yet another group drank draft beer from steins while they sang and shouted loud and cheerful toasts at passersby. Little girls in local costumes held on tightly to their mamas' hands or carefully carried baskets that had been filled with flowers and decorated with small flags or slogans. Guesthouses were doing a brisk business, and vendors in food booths barked out their specialties. The sweet-sour aroma of steamed sauerkraut and clouds of smoke rising from sizzling brats and knackwurst browned on hot grills made me hungry. I took my place in the long line and waited until the vendor cheerfully took my money, and then I relished the taste of the juicy brats and dripping sauerkraut squeezed between a crackling hard roll.

When I arrived at Boderbauer's shop, Bertl, Inge, and Karola were already waiting for me.

"Here she comes."

"You are always late, Anneliese."

"I'm not the only one who is late. Where is Mary?" I asked.

"She can't come." Karola explained, "She has to march in the parade with her mama and papa."

Bertl nodded. "Yes, my mama said Mary's papa and mama are party members now, and they will be something big in the party soon."

The sound of the bands approach startled us and we scrambled for a front spot on the sidewalk. Burgomaster Kegler, the mayor, and the regional director of the Socialist Arbeiter Partei or Socialist Worker's Party (SA) led the parade. Then came the ten-year-old members of Hitler's Young Folk organization, then the Hitler Youths, ages twelve to sixteen, and finally the SA. Most of the adults we knew didn't use either title, they just called them the "Brown Shirts."

The brown shirts and brown short summer pants worn by the Hitler Youth differed only slightly from the uniforms of the SA. The SA members wore hard rimmed visored caps with small eagle patches sewn to the fronts. On the left upper arm they wore an arm band with the miniature emblem of the national flag. Long, brown knickerbockers tucked into knee-high, black leather boots completed their uniforms. These men commanded respect, and we stood in awe as their legs came up and their boots became one black line rigidly snapping on the cobblestone streets, ka-rak . . . ka-rak, while their arms swung forcefully back and forth.

The SA units also sang with stirring gusto. Germany's popular song, commemorating the sacrifice of those who fought for the Fatherland and gave their lives, echoed from the walls,

> I had a comrade, a better one you won't find.
> The drums called us to fight,
> and he walked by my side,
> he marched in step with me.
> He marched in step with me.
>
> A bullet whizzed by us.
> Was it for him? Was it for me?
> It tore him from my side - - -
> before my feet he lay,
> as if he were a part of me.
> As if he were a part of me.

We applauded each group as they marched by singing their favorite song. Sometimes we hummed along and we watched as the older people waved with one hand and wiped tears from their cheeks with the other. Yet, there were others who looked on in stony silence.

"Oh, there is Mary and her mama and papa," I said.

Mary smiled and waved excitedly. Rosa, Mary's sister, was ahead of her family and strutted along, proud as a peacock, while she turned her head left and right. She drew attention to her tiny waist by wearing the black belt extra tight.

"Just look at her," said Inge. "She acts like she is the only League of German Maiden member in the world."

"Her new uniform does look sharp, doesn't it?" I sighed, "I just love her uniform. Don't you?"

We had to admit, in her uniform, Rosa looked much better than we did. Her snowy-white blouse had two breast pockets and it contrasted sharply with a black kerchief. The kerchief, skillfully folded in the regulation triangle, rested on her shoulders and a brown, woven leather ring held the tie ends in place at the nape of the neck.

The dark-blue skirt of military cut covered her legs to mid-calf. She wore white anklets and special marching shoes.

We waved eagerly and shouted, but Rosa ignored our good wishes because Rosa did not know us today.

Bertl pointed. "Look how tightly she wears her belt."

"I bet she has to hold her breath most of the time," I replied.

"I hope she bursts the buckle and drops her skirt," Karola snapped.

The bearers of the party's standards caught our attention. I could hardly breath, all these colors! I whispered, "Oh, this is wunderschoen!"

Each square standard was framed by a narrow white, and a wide black border. The red background in the four corners had a golden eagle perched on a miniature swastika and the white inner circle set off the Nazi symbol. The black swastika was encircled by a ring of gold oak leaves. Row upon row of flag bearers was lost in the forest of walking flags fluttering softly in the wind.

The labor force had an honor group of sixteen-year-old Land Year girls who had completed a year of compulsory work on a farm. Then came the Household girls who had chosen to help mothers who had four or more children. Each group carried a flag or the slogan, "The Fuhrer will command and we will follow."

Young men called the "Soldiers of Work" or the National Labor Service organization marched proudly by. The cleats of their boots had cut the grass until the cobblestones looked green and shiny. Two members of the Labor Service carried their slogan, "Blood and Soil."

Mrs. Sollfrank, who stood right behind us, said to her neighbor, "There is Heiner, my youngest. The Labor Service made him grow up, and it was the best thing that ever happened to him. He acts like a man now, and he is much easier to live with. In three months he will be home and then he can go on with his life and put to use what he has learned."

"My Alfred says that the Nazi party is getting a year of cheap labor. All of these young people are working for almost nothing," said her neighbor.

"Yes, but just look at them," another woman replied. "They look so healthy. Those boys needed to learn how to do something for their country. Frau Solfrank is right, now they will know how to work. They had a lesson that will last a lifetime."

We had never seen so many farmers' wives and daughters in their regional taffeta or brocade costumes. They wore hats or caps trimmed with delicate laces and pearls, and the design of their dresses was adapted to the history of their villages. The men were dressed in costumes handed down through generations. Their vests and jackets were clasped together by chains of gold or silver coins that signified the status of the owners and the size of their farms. They sang ballads and waved to the crowd with their fancy walking sticks. These sticks had hand-carved, intricate designs and held the inlaid or attached medals and coins won by the owner in various contests. The grandpas had washed and trimmed their white beards and some, for this occasion, smoked fragrant tobaccos in long, hand carved pipes. The elaborate patterns of their smoke rings fascinated and entertained the crowd. Factory and business owners who followed smiled and beamed as they led their labor groups down the street.

Finally, a large banner appeared with the slogan, "We Are the Future of the Fatherland." As the huge banner passed, we saw Hitler Youths who pushed small wagons filled with toddlers of prominent party members while preschoolers walked along side. Some children smiled, while others cried because they did not want to sit still and wave their tiny flags.

The parade held everyone's interest until the last row of participants had passed. We watched, and we couldn't understand why several people quietly withdrew from the ranks of the big crowd and left.

"We are not leaving this parade, we will stay," determined Bertl.

"Come on," I urged, and we followed the marching units into the market square where the Burgomaster, an eloquent speaker, approached the podium. In his speech, he took us back to 1918, the Olden Days, when things were bad. He told us that six million workers, family men, had been out of work for seven years. His father had been one of them, but in 1923 his father had found work, and he earned millions of marks every day. No one would believe it now, but then, millions of marks were needed because a loaf of bread cost one billion marks. Workers brought money home by the cartloads, but they couldn't even buy a newspaper because it cost two billion marks.

"How many millions make a billion marks?" Karola whispered.

The mayor's voice rose. "The only people who could support their families were the bankers and the factory owners. I remember when workers were chattel, hired and fired at will. They had no hope. They lived in housing for the poor, and one meal a day at soup kitchens kept them and their families from starvation."

The older people applauded and nodded in agreement as the Burgomaster finished his speech and returned to his chair.

"My father was out of work for five years, and we lived in the House of the Poor," Mr. Hoofer called out. "When we were sick, we had no heat, and no money to get a doctor. I'll never forget."

As the regional leader came to the podium, everyone applauded wildly. He was a well-known war hero of World War I, and the right side of his jacket was bedecked with rows of medals. He motioned to the crowd and waited patiently until everyone was silent.

He told us that he spoke as the voice of the Fuhrer, and he too, reminded everyone of the time when Germany was down and out. But then his voice rose, "For the past two years, Adolf Hitler has proven that he will make our Fatherland strong. It was he who brought the state of Saarland back to us. Now, we have coal mines and there is work for everyone in that region." He looked up to heaven and told, "Providence gave us Adolf Hitler and with our support, he will build a Reich that will last a thousand years."

As if by command, the SA members rose, raised their right arms in the Nazi salute and shouted, "Heil Hitler! Heil Hitler! Heil Hitler!"

Moved by the rhythmical, passionate drone of the SA, the crowd rose, row after row. Inge, Karola, Bertl, and I jumped to our feet and joined in shouting, "Heil Hitler! Heil Hitler! Heil Hitler!"

The regional commander extended his hands and bade us to listen, but the fervor was contagious, hearts pounded wildly in the fire of enthusiasm. "Heil Hitler! Heil Hitler! Heil Hitler!" The sound of our cheers echoed throughout the town square.

As the speaker continued, the audience began to listen again. "I am not finished with my message from the Fuhrer. Adolf Hitler

Two billion marks - the cost of a newspaper.

said that he is going to put every able-bodied man to work. Every working family, especially those with three or four children, are eligible to sign up and buy a 'Siedlung Home.' Herr Burgomaster Kegler has already signed the papers for the construction of seventy-four modest, affordable family homes on the outskirts of town. Our Fuhrer believes that every family has the right to own a home."

Shouts of, "Yes! Yes!" rang forth.

The speaker motioned to the crowd for quiet. "Every family should save, and in four years or less, each family can be the proud owner of a Volkswagen."

Again, the audience cheered, "We want a home, a car! Heil Hitler!"

Some listeners hugged, others pounded each other on the back, and all applauded wildly. Bertl looked at me, but I was busy jumping up and down, clapping and cheering. The idea of Papa and Mama having a car was wonderful.

Bertl and I jumped in anticipation. "Wunderbar! Wunderbar! Just think, someday we can go everywhere," she called out.

"I go to Berlin with Papa," I joined in. "I will ask Papa if I can join the Hitler Jungmaiden."

"I join, too!" Bertl shouted.

The regional leader went on. "Dr. Speer is already building the Autobahn, a network of super highways, that will join one border of Germany to the other. Look around you! There isn't another country in the world that has an Autobahn like our Fuhrer is building for us. But that is not all. The organization 'Strength through Joy' provides thousands of vacations for our workers. We must work hard to lay the foundation for the 1000 Year Reich. To our Fuhrer, Adolf Hitler, Heil Hitler!"

A chorus of, "Heil Hitler, Heil Hitler, Heil Hitler," resounded throughout the market square. The church bells rang and the generally reserved people of the Oberpfalz region went wild with enthusiasm. It was such fun to jump and shout and not be told, "Sit still and be quiet!"

Someone near the speaker's podium stood up and called out, "Three years ago I didn't have a job. I didn't have a home. Now I have both! Someday I'll get me a car! Heil Hitler!"

We again were consumed by a wave of emotional frenzy.

Photo of the models of the best, affordable Siedlung homes built during 1934-35, after Adolf Hitler's rise to power. Siedlung homes of lesser quality and size were also built, but families who could doument their Aryan blood-line and had proof of unblemished work ethics, could apply for the homes shown. These homes were built throughout Germany and if the homes were not destroyed during the war, they are still owned by the families who purchased them during 1934-1939.

Adolf Hitler appointed Dr. Speer to build Autobahn network to connect all of Germany. This massive undertaking reduced unemployment: 1933 - six million workers were unemployed. By January 1936 unemployment was reduced to two million five hundred thousand, and by 1939, three hundred and two thousand workers were unemployed.

However, the millions of young people, who worked as Soldiers of Work, or Land Year workers earned below living standard wages during their year of service. (I earned 15 marks per month.)

Left: Gas station on the Autobahn.

Choruses of "Heil Hitler, Heil Hitler, Heil Hitler" rose once more.

The speaker had finished with a flourish and the audience's energy and enthusiasm were spent. For a moment, silence fell over everyone and everything. The town band struck the first chord to the national anthem. As if on cue, the crowd stood and hundreds of arms raised in the German salute. Our national anthem echoed from the rooftops and the walls of the homes towering over us. Droning drums, the trumpets hitting the high notes, and the multitude of blending voices sent shivers through me and I felt goose bumps all over. Every beat of music lifted my spirits, and I believed every word I had heard.

After the national anthem, a party member from the National Labor Party spoke. "Now let us honor our work forces who are the movers of our nation. Follow me to the town hall where we will erect the Maypole in their honor."

A delegation of the various labor groups had selected the most majestic fir tree in our district. The May tree, felled by hand and stripped of its bark, towered high into the air. Garlands and three wreaths shaped from the branches of the tree adorned the Maypole, and each trade union nailed its carved emblem to the tree's trunk. The mayor and the regional director of the SA lifted the first spade of earth from the hole used for the erection of the Maypole. Selected men from the labor groups hoisted the Maypole into place while co-workers shouted.

"Come on, Franz."

"Get with it, Max."

"All right, Willi, show us how it is done!"

"More to the right, Joseph. No, no, not so far."

"Once more, you fellows! A one, a two, hie, ho, let's go! Up, up, up, good, a little straighter. Good."

Everyone cheered and clapped as the Maypole finally came into position. The workers filled in the big, deep hole and tamped the dirt to make sure the Maypole stood securely. It was no secret that the competing labor groups from the surrounding towns had delegated someone to spy and that these spies watched diligently. If they could steal a rival group's Maypole during any given night in May, they would. Members of our Youth Labor union watched and prevented such shame because a town without a Maypole was unthinkable.

The labor leader challenged, "Is there anyone here who is man enough to steal our Maypole?"

Everyone was silent.

"All right," he continued, "since there are no takers, bring on the dancers."

The audience moved back and welcomed the regional dance group. Young women dressed in traditional dirndls pirouetted, bowed, stepped back, and bade the male dancers to join them. The men wore black leather shoes, white knee-high socks, and short, black leather pants held up by leather suspenders. To complete their outfits, each wore a white, short-sleeved shirt and a black felt hat with a big, white plume. The men leaped high into the air, landed on their hands, and somersaulted until the spectators clapped and shouted for more. Then the young men faced each other and danced the Tyrolese clog dance. Mock slaps cracked on their partner's cheeks and each dancer propelled high into the air while he slapped his thighs and the leather soles of his shoes. Suddenly the men encircled their women who had stood aside. They whirled them around the Maypole while several dancers sang and yodeled. Some of the yodelers held the high notes until my skin tingled. They danced encore after encore for their appreciative audience until they were exhausted.

Finally, the mayor stepped up to the podium and announced, "The May Day parade is over, but the festivities of this special day will conclude tonight. The Maypole dance begins after sundown and the beer hall opens at eight. We, the residents of the town, invite all the adults to celebrate with us tonight. Until then, comrades, Heil Hitler."

People began to mill around and slowly they started to leave. Bertl, Inge, Karola, and I took leave of each other and looked for our parents. I suddenly realized I hadn't seen Mama and Papa nor Uncle Pepp and Aunt Sofie at the parade. The acquaintances whom I asked had not seen them either.

"Come to think of it, I haven't seen them." Frau Miller said. "Why, no one should miss a May Day celebration like that!"

"Mama and Papa stayed home because Mama doesn't feel well," I interjected.

"Must have come on rather sudden. I saw her working last night with Mr. Engelman. She didn't look sick to me," she retorted.

Suddenly, I felt so alone. I broke into a run. I had to get home so I could tell Mama and Papa what a wonderful parade they had missed. Oh, what a great day this was! Entranced by what I had heard and seen today, I vowed that I would find a way to join the Young Maiden organization so I could do something for my country. I felt so great and I was so proud to be a German girl.

Sister Resi (4 years) and I (9 years)
Around 1935

(A woman must know:)

Din frau muß wißßen:

(When a store is pure Aryan.)

Wann ist ein Geschäft rein arisch?

(When the Capital - the personnel the owner and the manager are pure Aryan)

Wenn Kapital
Personal
Inhaber
Geschäftsführer
rein arisch sind.

Wenn die Leitung des Geschäftes nicht in Händen eines Juden sich befindet und den Einkauf nicht ein Jude tätigt.
Wir erfüllen nachweislich alle diese Punkte!
Karlauf, der erfahrenste Fachmann, kauft selbst ein.
Bau auf

KARLAUF K.G.
NÜRNBERG-A. KAISER STR. 9

(Slogan: "If you buy from Jews, you stab the Fuhrer in the back.")

CHAPTER THREE

CHANGES

Papa acted strange tonight. He was not in the living room, nor was he sitting in his chair reading the paper like he always did. Instead, he was in the kitchen with us. He paced back and forth, he looked out the window, he paced again, before he turned toward Mama.

"Peppi, when did you say they'd be here?"

"Martin Hubner said he and Herman Brant will be here at seven, tonight, and I should make sure that you would be home also. By the way, Martin was wearing his SA uniform."

"Are they coming to talk about the new school?" Papa asked.

I turned to Papa and pleaded. "Papa, Mary said it won't cost anything to go to that school, and Inge said that they won't have the nuns to teach them anymore. I want to be with my friends. Please, may I go to the Peoples' School? May I?"

The door chimes sounded and Papa turned to me, "Anneliese, you be quiet now, you hear?"

He opened the door and Mister Hubner and Herman Brant stepped into view. As if on command, they brought the heels of their shiny black boots together and raised their right arms in the Nazi salute. "Heil Hitler! Max, Peppi, you were expecting us, were you not? Our concern is the future of your children."

Though we had known Mister Hubner for years, tonight in his uniform he looked different. His SA cap covered his pitch black hair, but nothing could hide his bushy eyebrows. They stood out like black wires and the fatty pockets around his lower eyelids partially hid his big, brown eyes. Mister Hubner smiled a lot. This caused the tightly pulled straps of his SA cap to embed themselves in the rolls of his flesh that pushed his red, puffy cheeks toward his nose while his double chin protruded over the collar of his shirt and hid his stubby neck. His broad shoulders and the huge buckle of the SA uniform belt accentuated his short frame and stockiness.

Herman was much younger than Mama and Papa, and he looked so sharp in his SA uniform. He always said that his blond hair and blue eyes proved that his forefathers were one hundred percent Aryan.

"Max, Peppi, do you remember Herman?" Mister Hubner asked.

"Come in," Papa said, motioning them toward the living room.

Mama stopped briefly. "Anneliese, I will check on little Max, but you and Resi go upstairs and get ready for bed. Now!" Hastily she added, "Sleep well." With that she closed the door.

I turned to Resi. "Do you want to go to first grade at the Witness School next year?"

"What's that?" she asked wrinkling her brows.

"That's the school we go to now where we have the Sisters as teachers. Next year, we could go to the German Peoples' School, that is, if Papa signs," I explained.

"I like Sister Anna, she lets us play with paper and she lets us sew and cut with real scissors. I want to go to her school."

I could see that Resi would be of no help. I tucked her in and turned out the light. Wide awake, I tossed in my bed until I couldn't stand it any longer. I needed to know what took place, so I tip-toed past Resi's door and moved quietly to the foyer. The coldness of the stone tile penetrated the soles of my feet and made me shiver. Gingerly, I crouched down behind the partly open foyer door and listened to Papa's steady voice.

"Herman, Martin, as I said before, Peppi and I will rear our children the way we feel is best. We have nothing against anyone, but that is the way we feel and that is the way it will have to be."

"Well, Max, then we leave. We did approach you, though."

I moved hastily and rushed up the stairs. My heart pounded wildly as I sought safety under the down cover and thought, "What did Papa mean when he said, "That's the way we feel, and that's the way it will have to be?" He always said that to me when I asked him why he would not join the Nazi Party. I never understood his reasons when he said that to me. As I drifted off to sleep, I wondered if Mr. Hubner and Herman understood what Papa meant.

I sat up with a start. It was past eight in the morning, and this was the first vacation day I could remember where Mama had not called me for church service. That could be a good sign since the Peoples' School did not check on church attendance. Quickly, I rushed downstairs and entered the kitchen.

"Good morning Papa. Good morning, Mama," I said cheerily. "I am going to the Peoples' School next fall, aren't I?"

They looked at each other. Neither smiled. Papa took my hands, "No, Anneliese, we told Mister Hubner that we will enroll you in the Witness School."

"The Witness School?" I gasped. "Papa, why do I have to go there when no one else will go there! I want to go to school with my friends and a regular teacher. At the Witness School I will be with all the girls from the villages."

Papa took me by the arm and said sternly, "Erna will go to the Witness School and I know there are others, too."

"Erna will have Ida to go with her," I argued.

"No, Anneliese, Mister Hubner told us that her father joined the Nazi Party last night, so Ida, Johan and little Karl will attend the Peoples' School."

"See? Everyone is going there! Why can't we be like everyone and join the Nazi Party, too? Mary told me that her papa thinks people should wake up, get smart and know what's good for them. Please let me go to school with my friends, and then I can join Hitler's Maidens Organization, too."

"No, for you, that will not be. Our decision stands."

Papa was still holding my hands while tears flowed down my cheeks. I jerked free from his grip and cradled my head on the table and cried loudly.

Mama came toward me with a bowl of steaming oatmeal. "Anneliese, come, eat your breakfast," she coaxed, "you will feel better."

"I'm not hungry and I will never feel better and I am not eating. I'll just stay hungry until I get sick. Then I won't have to go to school at all."

"Stop that!" Papa snapped. "Go to your room and cry there. While you are up there, make your bed and then come back."

I slammed the door to my room, threw myself on the bed, sobbed, and rubbed my eyes until they hurt. Thinking of Papa, I pounded my pillow.

Resi tugged at my nightgown. "Anneliese, why are you doing that?"

"Go away! Go downstairs, go to the Witness School and cut paper," I shouted. She moved away from me and left quietly.

I vowed to stay in my room all day, but then Uncle Pepp came. I rushed downstairs. He, Mama, and Papa were in the kitchen talking.

"Karl never said a word to me about joining," I heard Uncle Pepp say. "Everyone says it is good for the bakery, but I never thought he would join without saying a word to us. Even Mother had to hear it in the store. Did he say anything to you? I thought maybe he said something to you, Max?"

Papa shook his head. "No, I heard it from Martin last night. It caught me off guard."

Uncle Pepp slammed his fist on the table. "That's family for you. I had to hear it in the store because my cousin can't face me and tell me."

"Well, it's done and there isn't anything we can do about it. It is his family, Pepp. Leave it alone," advised Papa.

"Mama, may I go to see Bertl?" I asked.

"All right, but be home for dinner. I am making Papa's and your favorite meal, rouladen and noodles."

Long-faced and unhappy I dragged along the road. What if none of the parents of my classmates sent their children to the Witness School?

Mary, Inge, and Karola were already at Bertl's home. "Anneliese, Papa told me that your papa didn't sign you up for the Peoples' School." Mary called out. "Why?"

"I will have to go to the Witness School because Resi wants to go there."

"Then you can't come with us during summer vacation." Mary continued. "Rosa and I will go to a Hitler Youth camp, and then we will stay for two weeks on the North Sea during Papa's party training session. I can't wait! We have never been anywhere. Papa said, 'Our Fuhrer loves children and he is good to us'"'

"When I get home, I will ask if I can go, too." Inge interrupted. "I bet I can. Bertl, did your papa sign you up?"

"No, Papa didn't sign me up. If he can buy the hotel he wants, we are moving to Munich."

Karola was unhappy. "I just knew that Mama wouldn't sign," Karola complained, "so now I won't know where I will go until Papa comes home from his sales trip."

Mary named a whole litany of people who, according to her papa, had signed their children up for the Peoples' School. "Just think, boys will be in the same building with us, and we won't wear our old, ugly school uniforms, but for special days we will wear our beautiful Hitler's Maiden uniforms."

The coming school year would hold numerous exciting experiences for my friends, and they would always go without me. I felt so isolated. Before they would see the tears that welled up within me, I got up to leave. I didn't think I could feel any worse, but I did when they didn't even coax me to stay. During Easter vacation I stayed close to home and mourned my fate. Papa always spoiled everything for me. Each day passed slowly, and I dreaded going to the Witness School.

The Catholic Witness School had been moved into the vacated Lutheran school which had three classrooms fit for use. Two grades were crowded into each room, and with strict discipline, learning and achievement still their priorities, the Sisters managed. But Karola and I hated being there because we were the easy targets of the Peoples' School students.

They taunted, "Now don't you turn into good little Lutherans, that wouldn't do, would it? Only dumb students like you, who don't know where they should be, go to school on Saturdays." Then they cajoled, "Wouldn't you sooner go on a hike with us, or do you really like to go to school on Saturdays?"

We attended school on Saturday mornings and helped the sisters clean the rooms and halls, but all the while we longed to be with Mary and Inge. I was still angry with Papa and I couldn't understand why he wouldn't join the Nazi Party when the Party provided many advantages for its members. We watched as Mary's and Inge's parents moved into their new Siedlung homes. These new brick houses with red slate roofs cropped up like mushrooms on the outskirts of town. Each new Siedlung house was painted beige, but the owners used their individual talents and gave their home its own identity. Some added shutters and flower boxes, while others designed beautiful flower beds and tended productive vegetable gardens. Manicured rose hedges separated the homes and gave each family the privacy it sought. The young men of the National Labor Service, the Soldiers of Work, moved party members to their new homes, and they sang old favorite folk songs while they marched to their work stations. They cleaned long-neglected irrigation ditches, planted trees, and created new hiking trails in the surrounding forests. Even Sundays brought excitement. The troops of the National Labor Service challenged the teams of the surrounding areas for afternoon soccer matches.

There were other changes, too. Fewer and fewer people attended the worship services. Father Neidl admonished, "Remember, we need God's help not only when we are down and in trouble. Now more than ever, we should praise God and ask him to guide us always to make the right choices."

The students of the Peoples' School rarely attended church. Frequently, during Sunday masses, the Hitler Youth Organizations assembled at the Market square where they played their instruments loudly and sang as they took off on scheduled Sunday excursions. Rosa, Mary's sister, told us she didn't feel it was wrong to miss church.

"How can I go to church when the party members hike almost every Saturday and come home late? Sometimes we stay for the weekend because Mama and Papa have adult meetings and training sessions. We meet people from all over, and they too are busy working for the Fatherland."

We reminded Rosa and Mary not to forget what Father Hepfner had taught us. "Skipping a Sunday church service is a mortal sin, and anyone who dares to miss will burn in Hell forever."

"Not when you do good work for others, and for your country," Rosa replied. "Besides, we surely do keep the Fifth Commandment when we fulfill our Fuhrer's command, 'One for all, and all for one.'"

Secretly, I wished that Papa would let me join the party, but I knew there was no use asking again because he wasn't home, and Mama was upset and anxious. She had gone to Mister Freiman's store to buy yarn for our knitting class. Several SA men fastened posters to the store windows as others stood near the entrance. "GERMANS DON'T BUY FROM JEWS," the posters stated. As Mama entered the store, an SA member took her picture. Mister Freiman told Mama that this had been going on all day and the leader of the SA group had asked the German sales personnel to leave.

Mama told Uncle Pepp when he stopped by, "I wish Max could work in town like other men. I never can talk things over with him when I need to know what to do. Why did they take my picture?" "Peppi, I will tell you what I tell my customers. For generations, everyone in town has bought from the Freiman and Klein clothing and variety stores because they have quality and service. Just watch, the SA won't do much harm because they don't have the nerve. Did you realize that the SA men exchange towns with it comes to the Jewish business? The SA men from here go to the Jewish stores in Marktredwitz, and the SA men from Marktredwitz come here to harass the Jewish store owners and their customers. They must have lots of pictures of women and children. It seems to me they lack character and courage. There has been no direct confrontation from them, but they work behind your back. Just like Karl! He had to join them without a word to me or anyone else in the family. How could he do that, Peppi?"

"Pepp, Max doesn't like it either, but he says 'It is Karl's business what he decides.' We should leave him alone. Forget it, Pepp!"

"No, Peppi. I have always treated him up-front, but he went behind my back." Uncle Pepp vowed, "Maybe you and Max won't say anything. I won't have it! By God, I won't forget. Never. Never!"

CHAPTER FOUR

THE ARYAN

I was so excited and proud because Papa I thought wanted to talk with me about school. Mama made sure Resi could play with her friends, Max was sleeping in his crib, and now I was all alone with Papa and Mama.

"Anneliese, you are almost ten," Papa said. "Mama is concerned, so listen."

Papa and I listened intently while Mama spoke. "Max, I told Pepp I just don't know how to handle the new rules the SA puts out. Have you seen the posters at the Freiman's and Klein's stores? 'GERMANS DON'T BUY FROM JEWS.' These men even tell children to stay out of the stores because the owners are Jews and every public announcement box at the market square and along the streets has daily bulletins on the fight against Jews. The newspaper articles and radio news broadcasts repeat the same topic over and over again, so Anneliese comes home full of stories and questions. I told her that she should listen to what you have to say."

She turned toward me. "Anneliese, now listen carefully to your papa."

"Peppi, I read signs on my way home from Nuremberg. The signs assure customers that the store owners hired Aryan staff while Jews with expertise in business and professions are laid off. Other store signs state 'Only traitors buy from Jews,' or 'If you do business with a Jew, you stab our Fuhrer in the back.'"

"I have seen signs, too, Papa."

"Anneliese, don't interrupt," Mama admonished.

"I don't know where this is going," Papa continued. "Mister Liebl, our Jewish branch engineer, thinks this is a tactical thing with the SA right now and it will pass after they have drawn attention to their party. I just don't know."

"What will we do, Max?'

"Let's not get into that now, Peppi. I heard from Pepp that the Freimans are emigrating to America, and Mister Klein's wife is a Roman Catholic and she is one hundred percent Aryan so there isn't much they can do to him, is there?"

"But Papa," I interrupted. "Rosa and Mary told Bertl it's about time our Fuhrer gets rid of the Jews because they are like poison mushrooms and if we are not vigilant they will poison us. Rosa and Mary said that they don't know why the **STURMER** newspaper isn't in our school. In Nuremberg the teachers and students read it every week and they learn the truth about the Jews. Their mama and papa always buy the **STURMER** newspaper and Rosa showed us the articles and pictures. It tells that the Jews hate us and that they will kill us any way they can."

"Anneliese . . ."

"But Papa, there is more!" I continued. "Mary has a new reading book and she learned this poem,

'Don't trust a Jew's oath anymore than you
would trust a fox on a green meadow.'

She showed me another long poem, but I forgot most of it. It says that Jewish teachers can't teach us anymore. Mary also said that her papa thinks that we should remember, especially since we are Catholics... it was the Jews who killed Jesus."

"Now, Anneliese, I hope you don't believe everything you hear."

"Why not, Papa? This is in a real book, not a fairy tale book. Mary's papa has the book that tells all about the Jews and what they have done to us already. Mary's papa thinks our town is lucky because we're almost a pure Aryan town. We have only two Jewish store owners."

I turned toward Mama. "Mama, could Mister Freiman put that mushroom poison in candy and poison us?"

"Anneliese, you won't be poisoned by anyone. You will be all right."

"Papa, if I can't buy my books and things at the Freiman or Klein store, do we have to go to Waldsassen or Marktredwitz? Rosa

See
Page 28
Paragraph 4

See
Page 28
Paragraph 7

and Mary's mama and papa buy there from pure Aryan stores because that is where the faithful Germans buy."

"Anneliese, as I said, your Mama will do the buying. You will be all right. Now listen and do what I say." Papa took my hands. "If you see Mister Klein or Mister Freiman on the street, I expect that you will be polite. You understand?"

"Yes, Papa. But why is everything so different? Mary said that we should really hate the Jews for trying to poison us. Don't you think we should?"

Papa was angry and he pulled me toward him. His eyes penetrated my being and his hands gripped my shoulders. "Don't you ever hate," he said. "Hate is a terrible thing, so we don't hate anyone. Some day you will learn that hate makes you a lesser person than the person you hate. Now you listen to me, not to your friends, or anyone else. Anneliese, learn this, and remember it always. You will not hate Mister Klein, or anyone! You may dislike someone for what he or she does, but I will not hear that word ... hate ... in our home. Is that clear? I expect that you will behave and be courteous with anyone, but especially with Mr. Klein and Mr. Freiman or you will face my consequences."

"Yes, Papa. I will be good. I promise."

"Now also remember this," Papa said sternly. "I told Mama that you are growing up. I expect that you learn from listening to adults, but never forget that what you hear discussed in this house is only for the ears of the family. That means that you will tell not your friends or anyone else. If you have questions, you ask your mama or me, or Uncle Pepp, or Erna. I trust you can do what we tell you."

As Papa released me from his grip, my thoughts were spinning. I still didn't understand why Papa was so angry with me when I had told him the truth. I had told him what I heard about the Jews. A week later, I saw Mister Klein. He was not visiting with anyone who passed by. Maybe his attire startled them like it startled me. He wasn't wearing his black suit. He wore old work clothes and on the upper part of the shirt sleeve he wore a yellow band with a black star in the middle. He stooped forward here and there, and with wide, sweeping motions he pushed dung onto a shovel and held it in place with a whisk broom until he threw the waste into a wheel barrel.

I walked slowly past him and stammered awkwardly, "Good

day, Mister Klein. Why are you sweeping dung?"

Mister Klein didn't look up. I stood still and waited, but he just kept sweeping and in a hushed voice said, "Go, Anneliese. Go away this instant."

"But Mr. Klein, why are you wearing that star on your arm?

"Go, go, now, and ask no more!" he urged. "Now go!"

I walked to the other side of the street. All this time I wanted to know why Mister Klein wasn't in his store. I stood and watched as the older people walked by without saying a word to him. I couldn't understand it. I had been polite, like Papa had said I should be so I just waved to Mister Klein and walked on.

Mister Klein swept a different street each day and I was glad when he finished cleaning the streets in our neighborhood. Before long, it didn't seem so strange anymore; Mister Klein was just there, sweeping the streets, but I wondered why I never saw Mister Freiman.

I asked Uncle Pepp, "What happened to Mister Freiman? Where is he sweeping the streets?"

Uncle Pepp said, "Mister Freiman and his family left for New York, in America."

I wished Mister Klein would leave for America, too, so I would not have to see his stooped figure shuffling down the street, always sweeping dirt and dung.

After a while the Jewish store owners were forced to sell their businesses to Aryan families. The SA men left the store fronts and Mama could shop without having her picture taken. I was glad because everything was normal again.

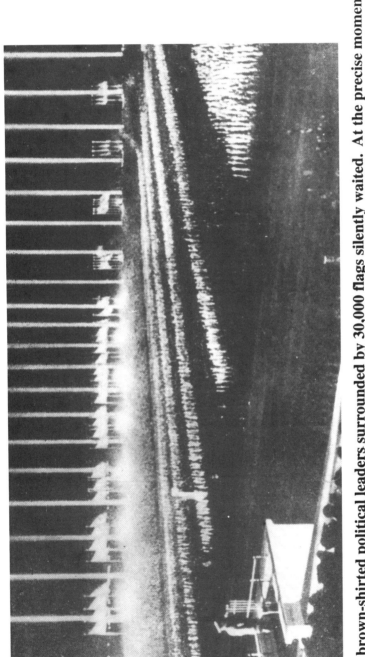

100,000 brown-shirted political leaders surrounded by 30,000 flags silently waited. At the precise moment of Adolf Hitler's entrance, 130 strobe lights encircled the Zeppelinfield in Nuremberg and then illuminated Adolf Hitler as he stood motionless on the elevated podium before he spoke. An English diplomat called the spectacular display the 'Cathedral of Éis', and he found that even the most skeptical members where momentarily spellbound.

CHAPTER FIVE

NAZI EXHIBITIONS OF POWER

As time passed, things got even better. Papa came home more often because Sager & Woerner, the company he worked for, was building a new Autobahn to Nuremberg. Frequently, I heard Papa and Uncle Pepp talking, and I loved to listen when Papa told about Nuremberg, because Nuremberg was now almost as important as Berlin.

"Pepp," said Papa, "I will admit that Hitler has kept his promise, and unemployment and soup kitchens are a thing of the past. Our firm was hosted a delegation from the Netherlands and England while they toured the Autobahn work site near Berneck. They were interested in our collapsible eating-and-living quarters that we move right along with our equipment, our work incentive options, and the socialized health benefits. They stayed at Strength-Through-Joy vacation spots until party officials asked the delegates to drive on the Autobahn to Nuremberg. At Nuremberg the group toured the Reichstag buildings and they were invited to return for the 1936 Reichstag celebration."

"I hear it will be the biggest one yet," Uncle Pepp said.

"Yes, the celebration gets bigger every year, and next year's celebration will surpass this one," Papa said.

"What are they building now?"

"The Zeppelin Field. Architect Albert Speer's plan calls for over 130 anti-aircraft flood lights to illuminate 100,000 uniformed party leaders, 30,000 flags, the heralding trumpets and the participating bands. Imagine what a sight that will be. I'm sure the movie theaters will show it during their weekly news reviews."

"All that money thrown away just for show," Uncle Pepp

pondered. "That's not good business."

"All I know is that 500,000 participants bring lots of work and business to Nuremberg and to all of Germany as well. You have seen for yourself, business is booming, and our company will do well this year."

But Papa said other things too. "Pepp, it looks so good, but, I can't go along with what the Nazi Party is doing to some people. Our senior engineer's son, Franz, attends an exclusive school that trains future Nazi Party leaders. Otto is worried that he lost his son to the Party because Franz denies his religious training, and he will do what is good for the Fatherland."

"Otto has an option," Uncle Pepp said. "Why doesn't he tell his son, 'You come home! You are through at that school.'"

"Otto knows it is too late for that. Franz has told him, ' If you order me to come home, I will go to the authorities and ask for permission to stay.'" Papa lowered his voice. "I have also heard that informers have given authorities names of business owners and residents because they are doing business or socialize with the Jews. The newspaper publishers and the National Socialistic German Workers Party bulletins print these names and then they ridicule and denounce anyone who associates with Jews. The SA party also rents spaces on public buildings to inform people who don't buy newspapers."

Uncle Pepp shook his head. "I just don't know how far they will go. I am glad we live in a small town where people know each other. We have Nazi members here too, but so far they have not bothered anyone too much. I guess we wait and see."

As Papa had told me, I kept his observations to myself, but I wondered: when Mary and Rosa's mama told their stories, they were forever praising Adolf Hitler. Rosa's mama told anyone who would listen, "Before our Fuhrer came to power, we couldn't afford a vacation. Matter of fact, we tried to find work during vacation so we could make ends meet, but now we can show Rosa and Mary our country. I'm so proud of my Otto! In his new position, he arranges vacations for young mothers who have at least four pre-school children. When they return, rested and tanned, they remark, 'For the first time in years we felt good because we could sleep through the night. We are grateful, and we will teach our children to serve our country."

Rosa was meaner than ever, and she gloated, "Mary and I are privileged because our mama and papa work for the Fatherland. Don't you forget it. We are special."

I didn't hate her, since Papa said that I couldn't hate anyone. I surely didn't like her, but secretly, Karola, and I wished that we could go to camp, too — and become leaders of the Jung Maidens.

CHAPTER SIX

CATCHING THE NAZI FEVER

After school started in the spring of 1937, news bulletins carried reports about the hikes and bus tours the Nazi Youth Groups and their leaders had taken. They held meetings and invited all ten-through fourteen-year-olds and their parents, whether the parents were Nazi Party members or not.

An elder SA member opened the meeting, "Next Saturday, we will care for your children from 6:00 a.m. to late evening. So pack noon lunch, and we will furnish the evening meal. We will give your children a day to remember. When they return home, listen to what they tell you. Heil Hitler!"

"Be sure you wear hiking boots," Mary told us. "Bring your knapsack, enough water, and lunch. Papa said that everyone should be grateful the SA is sponsoring such a glorious event for us. I do hope you come!"

I was glad that Papa wasn't home because I know he would say, "No, Anneliese, you are not going on that outing and that is that."

When I begged Mama to let me go, I couldn't believe it when she said, "Yes, you may go, I don't think it will do any harm."

All week long I was bubbling over with excitement. I buffed and oiled my hiking shoes, laid out my white knee highs, my white blouse and the navy-blue skirt. I didn't have a black kerchief like the Jung Maidens wore, but I was happy because I could go on the hike with them and my outfit looked almost like Mary's uniform.

Finally, it was Saturday. Dawn was chasing the night clouds away; only the rustling leaves of the chestnut trees broke the night silence.

At five, I went into Mama's room. "Mama, we can't

oversleep, you know.   I have to be there before six."

"Just slow down. Everything is set out, and I will fix your oatmeal right now. You pack your knapsack, and as soon as we see your friends, you may leave."

I had barely touched my oatmeal when Mary called out, "Anneliese, we are waiting!"

I dropped my spoon and grabbed the knapsack from Mama's hands and called out, "Good-bye, Mama," while I raced down to the garden path.

Mary and Karola jumped excitedly, "Come on, let's go!" they shouted.

We ran to the Hitler Youth Home just a block away. Promptly at six the leader called, "Attention! Everybody fall in. Ready? We are on the march to Wiesau."

Ten through fourteen-year-old boys, the Jungvolk marchers, carried flags or executed drum rolls, while others blew their trumpets announcing our approach. When our long column paused, we sang rousing marching songs.

> "Merry is the gypsy life
> Pharia, pharia phoom.
> We don't pay taxes to the Kaiser
> Pharia, pharia phoom.
> Here and there in the green forest
> There are our whereabouts
> Pharia, pharia, pharia
> Pharia, pharia pharia, phoom!"

We never tired. As soon as the last stanza of a song ended someone else called for a favorite. The singing made us feel good while we walked toward our destination. At Wiesau, we boarded the bus for the meeting area in the Waldnaabtal.

After we arrived, a young woman, highly decorated with several Nazi Party medals, stepped forward and welcomed us to the Waldnaabtal. Then, in a clear, vibrant voice , she led us in the Horst Wessel's song:

"The flags raise high,
the columns tightly closed.
SA marches with firm, determined steps.
Comrades, shot by the Red front and tribunal,
they march in spirit
within our columns now."

At the close, she motioned for silence and said, "I hope that some day everyone here may be called to be as brave as Horst Wessel. He served our Fuhrer Adolf Hitler. It was he who wrote the song and it was he who was shot by the Red front members while marching with his comrades."

The drummers beat their drums softly and the trumpets played a stirring, majestic dirge in memory of Horst Wessel. The leader then motioned for us to sit down. Several Jungvolk members and Jung Maidens stepped smartly forward, gave the Nazi salute and declared their loyalty to the Fuhrer and the Fatherland.

"I help with the collections of winter clothing for the poor."

"I read to the elderly who are in hospitals or homebound, and I also run errands for them."

"I serve willingly where help is needed and I do it proudly".

"I always do my best so our Fuhrer can be proud of me."

Several members then said, "We respect our leaders and we follow their examples."

The twin daughters of one of the leaders recited,

"My Fuhrer, I know you well and love you
like Papa and Mama.
I will always obey you,
as I obey Papa and Mama.
I shall bring you joy,
like the joy
I bring to Papa and Mama."

Their presentation set off thunderous applause. Following that, we took an imaginary Strength-Through-Joy trip. Each Berliner pretended to be traveling to a city in Bavaria. They tried to understand the dialects of our Bavarian regions as we gave directions to their destination. The transposition of vowels, the slurred contractions, and the absence of plural sounds confused them. No wonder they didn't understand us! As we traveled to Berlin, we had troubles with their dialect, too. The camaraderie and laughter grew with each skit and we learned that we, the Bavarians, and the rest of the country were very much alike. We now truly understood Adolf Hitler's cry of "One for all and all for one!"

During the late afternoon we played games, sat and talked. All this time I felt happiness I hadn't know for a long time. I belonged! Even Rosa was nice to me. I didn't understand it, but while we hiked, Mary explained.

"Mama said that if Rosa does not change her uppity ways, it will be her fault if we don't gain new Party members. Her attitude can cost us the trip to the Reichstag. If that happens, Mama said that she will be home scrubbing floors all year long."

The supper gong sounded, and we didn't have to be called twice. The aroma of the grilled bratwurst, hot cider and warm sourdough buns gave us a new spirit in our race for a place in line. As dusk enveloped the trees in twilight, the anticipation of the upcoming bonfire set us scurrying for wood. The wood, gathered and piled high, brought contentment of a job well done. As the last fiery orange strips of sky struggled and gave in to the night's command, an eerie calm settled over us. We waited while several leaders used long matches and kindled small branches until tiny tongues of flames licked the bark of the dry fir trunks, until one by one, the huge stumps broke and crumbled to the breathtaking energy of the fire. Enthralled, we looked on as the flames climbed up, eight ... ten ... twelve feet. Burning slivers of wood competed with the radiance of a falling star and the beauty of the night sky before they fell to the ground and turned to ashes.

The faces of the gathered group reflected in the flames' brightness. The flags took on a crimson redness and fluttered in the soft breeze, and the trumpets gleamed in a burnishing gold in the hands of the players. Suddenly, on command, the drummers beat their drums and the trumpet players stood tall, raised their trumpets and buzzed their lips for that high note. It came out clean and crisp, with a clarity that sent chills up and down my spine.

The elder SA leaders were an impressive sight with their black boots moving up and down, thumping the ground with each goose step. As the column of men reached the platform near the bonfire, they surged to attention with the Nazi salute. Slowly, the flag bearer moved forward and raised the Swastika flag until it fluttered from the tip of the mast.

After the drum roll, "Heil Hitler, Heil Hitler, Heil Hitler," resounded from the hills until it drowned the crackling of the huge fire. While the flames receded in the background, the troop leader reflected on the camaraderie we all had experienced on this day. He recounted striving for ideals expressed by the young speakers. He praised the feeling of belonging he had witnessed, and then he gave final tribute to our Fuhrer whose leadership made all of this possible. He went on to remind us that every good German should, no, *must*, belong to the party because unity and work are the foundation of a strong nation. Through unity and work, Germany regained respect — not just in Europe — but in the world as well.

"We will achieve new goals! We are on our way!" he emphatically shouted. Again, "Heil Hitler, Heil Hitler, Heil Hitler," reverberated throughout the forest with the sounds of unity and expectation. Then, the entire camp stood in somber silence as we remembered our fallen heroes, who, in the early 1930's, stood against the storm and fire of the Red opposition.

A group chanted, "They gave their lives willingly so we might live under the Fuhrer's leadership."

The red glow of the smoldering tree trunks mirrored the rapture on our faces as we joined hands and solemnly promised, "We will work for the Fuhrer. United we stand."

Then, with right arms raised, we sang the national anthem. "Deutschland, Deutschland Uber Alles" (Germany, Germany, above all). In that final moment one of the leaders reminded us to do what was right for the Fatherland.

"We will be one for all and all for one," he stated. After a pause, he said, "The day is done, the meeting adjourned."

Still mesmerized, we marched to the buses and all the way home we remained hushed. Some Jung Maidens slept. Others shared their thoughts in whispers. I looked out the window at the night sky, reliving the enchantment of the evening over and over in my mind.

Mama had waited up for me. "It's past your bedtime, Anneliese," she said, "Go to sleep. We'll talk in the morning."

"Good night, Mama," I mumbled. I was glad she did not ask questions now; I wanted to hang on to the events of the day and keep them alive until sleep overtook me.

The next morning, Mama listened intently while I recalled the events of the Saturday hike for her. "Mama," I pleaded, "I had so much fun. Why can't I be a Jungmaiden?"

"Anneliese, I am not going to discuss it with you now. I allowed you to go. Papa will talk with you and make the final decision when he comes home. Don't make me sorry that I let you go."

Papa and Mama stood firm. No matter how often I told them how wonderful I felt belonging for just one day, they just wouldn't listen. They couldn't possibly understand. But Mary understood, finally.

"Mama said that some people just need more time to see how good Adolf Hitler really is for us," she said. "It is up to us young people to show the older people what we can do."

After that, Mary invited me whenever the Jungmaidens had an invitational meeting.

When Cousin Hans heard about it, he said, "Anneliese, people like you and Karola are free-loaders. You go to invitational meetings, you have fun, but you don't join. That's not fair."

"I don't care what you say. You will never be a Hitler Youth because you are lazy and you are not as nice as a Hitler Youth should be," I retorted.

CHAPTER SEVEN

FALL HARVEST

As the long summer days gave way to fall, we looked forward to three days of October's potato vacation. Adolf Hitler said that all German youth must help to bring in the bountiful harvest and learn to honor the work of the farmer. Uncle Pepp made sure that we attended the morning church service before he took Erna, Lisl, Hans, and Hans' friend, Willi, and me to his potato fields where the hired farm hands worked hard already. On each end of the field Uncle Pepp placed baskets with freshly baked sourdough bread, hard rolls, a bowl of homemade cottage cheese, buttermilk, several thermoses of hot coffee, juice, and a bottle of beer for each man. The workhorses, Max, a bad-tempered, black stallion, and Fritz, a gentle, auburn mare, shook their heads and whinnied. With the "gad-dap" command a farm hand cracked the whip. White saliva bubbles dripped from their mouths as they started forward with a jerk, their heads bobbed and their shiny hooves scraped the topsoil. We stood and watched while the potato machine's iron teeth turned noisily, burrowed deep into the ground, and spewed the potatoes along the rows. Stooping down, we picked and placed them into the oblong wicker baskets.

At first, Cousin Hans and Willi, who emptied the baskets into sacks or onto the wagons, bragged about their masculinity. "You girls are so slow, it takes you forever to fill your baskets. We could have finished this row long ago if you weren't so weak and helpless."

By noon their bravado had reverted to, "If you girls didn't fill the baskets so full, we could work faster."

Sepp, Uncle Pepp's foreman, made sure that everything ran on schedule, that each worker did his part and picked each row clean. An hour before we stopped for the night, we collected the driest vines and piled them high for the main event of the day. We threw potatoes into the pile, and then we pestered Sepp until he gave in and lit the fire. Simultaneously, fires sprang up on the neighboring fields and in the hills, the smoke cast a bluish-gray veil over the land, and the aroma of the burnt vines and piping hot potatoes made our mouths water. We could hardly wait for the evening meal.

Finally, Sepp took a rake and retrieved the blackened potatoes and split them in half. The white meat inside steamed lustfully; we dabbed on off-white butter and watched it melt. We shared the lunch left overs, the women savored their strong, hot coffee, the men reached for their beer, and we enjoyed Babette's home-made currant juice. Late into the evening, Uncle Pepp came and right away he checked our work. We just knew he would find spots where we had to dig and retrieve even the smallest potatoes.

"Is that how you do your work in school?" he asked. "Well, that may be acceptable there, but not for me. You will go back and pick until the field is clean."

It was no use to grumble. Uncle Pepp checked each row until he was satisfied. Then he said, "Tomorrow, do it right in the first place. Now climb up on the potato wagon and I'll give you a ride home."

Liesl, Erna and I grabbed several empty sacks to cushion the lumpy spots and we huddled on the back of the wagon while Hans and Willi taunted.

"We don't need a ride, we'll walk with the farm hands. You girls are so soft, you just can't take hard work."

"Don't pay any attention to him," Lisl whispered. "You know how he is."

We passed fields where the workers were still picking and we felt good when we thought of our beds and rest.

"I'll never live on a farm," I said. "Every time, when I help in the fields, I hurt for days."

"It wasn't so bad today, but I hate it when it is cold and it rains just enough to make me miserable. Then I wish I could be in school instead," Erna concluded.

The wagon had reached our house. Mama stood by the garden gate and she called out, 'How was the picking, Pepp?"

"It was good, and we moved right along. We'll start the same time tomorrow."

"Good night, everyone," I called out as Uncle Pepp lifted me down from the wagon. It was so good to be home. I washed, crawled into bed, tossed and turned until I found the right spot for my aching bones and fell fast asleep. It felt like I had slept but a few minutes when Mama called me for another day of potato picking.

We returned to school, but fall harvest work continued until short, hard stubbles of straw were the only remnants in the wheat fields; the lush grass of the meadows stopped growing, and the plowed potato fields were straight, narrow rows of light-brown earth.

Before the first Sunday in Advent, Adolf Hitler spoke and asked that those who had all their needs met share their abundance with those who had less. Throughout the holiday season, into spring, most households pledged to limit themselves to a sparse, but nutritious "One Kettle Sunday Dinner." The SA members canvassed towns and villages for "voluntary" monetary donations which provided food, clothing, and improved housing for the needy. As the goal amounts were reached and surpassed, the SA members boasted, "Your generous giving enables our Fuhrer to lift his people up; now, even the poor can live with dignity. Again, our Fuhrer leads by caring even for those who have the least. He will keep his promises and make Germany a great nation."

CHAPTER EIGHT

ONE PEOPLE — ONE REICH — ONE LEADER

Germany pulsed with excitement and anticipation. Radios and loudspeakers blared throughout cities until our Fuhrer's voice interrupted the patriotic songs and spirited marches. "Austria has waited long enough! England and France must 'right a wrong'. They must abolish the 1918 Versailles Treaty and assist in the reunification of Austria with its homeland, Germany."

Then Adolf Hitler demanded the immediate resignation of the Austrian Chancellor, Schuschnigg. Enraptured, we listened while the radio announcers described the scenes from Austria, where hour upon hour, the people of Austria lined the sidewalks and blocked streets, chanting, "We want to return to the Reich!"

"One people! One Reich! One leader!"

On March 12, 1938, everyone in Germany was jubilant. England and France had come to terms. Radios were blaring and we listened as the descriptions of the events in Austria filled our homes. We read the newspapers, and my friends and I stood impatiently in line at the movie theater where we watched this important, historic event. Miraculously, overnight, cartons of swastika flags and Nazi symbols had appeared in Austria, and the vendors sold them to the eager takers. Now, these flags hid the sky in Salzburg and in the small mountain villages as they hung from home attics and arched the streets. Cheerful onlookers, squeezed tightly into the small spaces of their apartment windows, waved miniature flags or held unto bouquets of flowers. , In search of a good view, boys had climbed water fountains and lampposts and they skirted jubilant people who had lined the streets and sidewalks.

Cries of, "One people! One Reich! One leader!" filled the air.

Showers of flowers overwhelmed German SA units and military troops as they goose-stepped their way through the metropolitan areas to the villages of Austria. The most moving moment was the finale: Flags fluttered in the breeze while salutes and chants rose to a deafening roar as Adolf Hitler and his entourage entered Braunau. Overnight, our Fuhrer's birthplace had become a national shrine. During the twilight hours the motorcade arrived in Linz where our Fuhrer told hundreds of thousands of listeners that it was his destiny to return to his homeland and create the "1000 Year Reich." After the national anthem, everyone in the theater rose, shouted and clapped. Our Fuhrer had brought the Austrians home. Townspeople planned joyful reunions with their Austrian family members they hadn't seen in years. Uplifted, people praised the Fuhrer and credited him with the extension of Germany to its former borders. Within a month people settled down and dealt with daily chores and events. I looked forward to Easter vacation and everything was good, but not for long: No one believed it could happen, but it did.

THE CLOSING OF THE WITNESS SCHOOL

It wasn't long after Easter when Father Neidl took action and openly denounced the imminent closing of the Witness School.

He read to a startled congregation, "During 1938, it will be the Law of the Land for Germans of all denominations to send their children to the People's School." He paused and when he had everyone's attention, he went on. "You are aware that this law enforces the closing of the Witness School, and our Sisters of the Poor Franciscan Order will be without their respective teaching positions. After years of faithful service to our community they face forceful eviction."

Father Neidl reminded the congregation of the influence our Sisters had on almost everyone's life and asked, "What do you think you owe the Sisters who taught you and your children?"

The congregation came together as one. A farmer donated land to build a new home for the nuns while others tilled the ground for a huge vegetable garden, planted seeds and landscaped. Skilled craftsmen volunteered and worked on the structure while material and merchandise appeared miraculously. For weeks, but without success, frustrated Nazi officials tried to trace the cash and names of the many grateful citizens who had shown their appreciation.

Father Neidl was elated because the Sisters could stay close to their former work place and give private assistance to anyone who sought it. Mother Superior assured the congregation that their small pensions from the diocese, the vegetable garden, private tutoring and music lessons would sustain their frugal existence.

We who had attended the Witness School harbored mixed feelings about the changes before us. As young people, we were anxious to lose the label of Witness School students, but on the other hand, we were filled with the apprehension of joining a school system which we knew little about. For the first time, Nazi Party members would be our teachers, and male students would be attending classes nearby.

Once it was law, the transition from the Witness School to seventh grade in the People's School had no repercussions for us. We were reunited with former classmates who had known us since first grade. The special cliques we feared most were the members of the Nazi Party organization, but they felt so special and above us that they hardly acknowledged our existence. Like everyone, they were too involved with the stirring events that had changed our small town atmosphere.

THE SUDETENLAND

As of late, infantry and motorized units were stationed in our town, which faced the Czechoslovakian border. Families voluntarily lodged the solders in their homes, daily schedules were changed, and everyone tried to adapt. Cousin Hans and his friends gawked at the trucks and artillery units and talked about nothing else. We watched the sharp-looking soldiers and officers march by. They had shined their boots to a high gloss, their dress uniforms had knife-sharp creases, and the emblems on their caps glistened in the sun. They carried their rifles during precision marches, and they sang or shouted slogans.

My friends and classmates, Marerl, Karola and I, wished we were older. The soldiers spent their free evening hours walking or dancing with the young ladies while they ignored us.

The soldiers came to school, and in most serious tones they told us that our Fuhrer had ordered them to come to protect us and our town. Their talks focused on the causes of the present events and since we witnessed much of the present unrest, we listened and we understood.

Barely seven miles from our town lay the borders of the Sudetenland, where since the 13th and 14th centuries, 3.5 million Sudeten Germans lived and worked. After World War I, the Paris Peace Conference had created an independent Czechoslovakia, but of its 11.5 million citizens, 3.5 million were Sudeten Germans. The Czechs, we were told, constantly refused to recognize the cultural and economic contributions the Sudeten Germans had made and resentment against the Czechs smoldered within. Since 1931, the Sudeten Germans watched Adolf Hitler's rise to power. The growing internal strength of the Sudeten German Party, and the Annexation of Austria, torched numerous demonstrations under the slogan,"Home to the Reich!"

During the midweek of September 1938, airwaves resounded hour after hour with the frantic chant of the Sudeten Germans, "Home to the Reich!"

We heard Adolf Hitler's Munich speech, in which he angrily denounced the oppression of 100,000 Sudeten Germans who had fled the country and became fugitives.

"We must come home to the Reich," the fugitives chanted as they marched through the streets.

We went to the movie theater. Pictures didn't lie! We heard, we saw, and we believed. We watched in awe as statesmen Neville Chamberlin of England, Eduard Daladier of France, and our ally, Premier Benito Mussolini of Italy, landed in Munich to seek peaceful solutions to the growing threat of war.

Our Fuhrer stood firm. "The Sudentland must come home to Germany. We want to live in peace, but we are not afraid of war," he declared.

On September 29, 1938, over the strong objections of the Czechoslovakian President, Eduard Benes, the annexation of the Sudetenland agreement was signed by France and England. Our soldiers marched across the border into the Sudetenland, and the street scenes became a replay of Austria's annexation. The onlookers in the apartment windows high above and huge crowds that lined the streets chanted, "Home to the Reich! Home to the Reich!" And for hours, the chanting went on. "One people! One Reich! One leader!"

Everyone I knew was in agreement with Adolf Hitler's actions. When I asked Papa what he thought, he said, " Annexing Austria and the Sudetenland was a great coup of our Fuhrer because it made Germany bigger. Now the Sudeten Germans can visit us without restrictions, they can even live in our town, or they can reside anywhere in Germany."

Uncle Pepp, who had been sitting quietly nearby nodded his head. "I suppose now that we are one country, we can do more business with them and that should help everyone."

A GREATER, ARYAN GERMANY 1938-1939

The Sudetenland was not the last of Hitler's annexation. By spring 1939, Czechoslovakia became part of Germany. The Memelland, bordering on Lithuania, had belonged to Germany from the 17th century until 1918. On March 22, 1939, Lithuania surrendered this valuable territory with its ice-free harbor to Germany. On April 20, 1939, our Fuhrer's 50th birthday, towns throughout Germany competed. Our town outdid itself during the parade, the speeches and torchlight evening celebrations. They were constant reminders that it was our Fuhrer who had made Germany a great and powerful nation. I wondered if Papa would allow me to join the Young Maidens, if I did my best on my essay assignment and told everyone how I felt.

OUR FUHRER ADOLF HITLER

Immediately after World War I, Germany experienced its greatest poverty. Foreign countries took our resources, and the German citizens were abused and despised by these nations. It was 1919. Gas poisoned, an unknown soldier had lain in a field hospital and vowed that he would fight the oppression and free his Fatherland. This young man was our Fuhrer, Adolf Hitler. After his release, he joined the National Socialist German Workers' Party and he became the seventh member. Then he used the Party as a vehicle to make his plan a reality. Their meeting quarters were poorly equipped and small, but the members' determination for reform was fierce. The fiery speeches by the young soldier were the main reason for a steady increase in membership. The Party's greatest threat and opposition was the Bavarian rightist government led by Gustav Kahr.

Adolf Hitler came to a vital decision. He and his courageous party members marched up to the Munich Field Hall and supported the striking working class. As they neared the Munich Field Hall, sixteen loyal party members were shot by Kahr's troops and many were wounded. Considered by Kahr as a dangerous dissident, Adolf Hitler was imprisoned at the Landsberg fortress.

During his four-year incarceration, he wrote his book, **MEIN KAMPF**, where he expressed his thoughts on the question of the Jewish subjugation of the German people. It took many struggles and fights, but in 1933, our Fuhrer was elected our leader. Providence had rewarded Adolf Hitler's selfless sacrifices and made him the Fuhrer of the German nation.

I was so proud of the mark of "Excellent" on my essay. It had been so easy to write because I believed what I had written.

When I asked Papa if I could join the Young Maidens when I was fourteen, his answer was the same. "No, Anneliese, you may NOT join, and that is that!" When Papa said that phrase, I knew he would never change his mind. He told Resi and me that as of now, Mama needed our help more than ever because sometime during October a little brother or sister would join our family.

We were into August when once again, people witnessed Adolf Hitler's leadership. Germany and the Soviet Union had signed a nonaggression pact. With no more threat from the East, peace was assured. A few days later, though, Adolf Hitler boldly demanded, "The time has come for Poland to immediately annex to Germany, the free city of Danzig and its entire harbor territory. After all ninety-five percent of its people are Germans, and Danzig has belonged to

Germany from 1814 until 1918, after World War I."

Poland refused to meet our Fuhrer's demands, and instantly, England threatened, "We will enforce a sea blockade."

We could sense the uneasiness of the adults. They met on street corners, in guesthouses and at home and wondered out loud. "Has our Fuhrer pushed too far this time? Are we on the brink of war?"

Hitler reviewing his troops before going to war.

CHAPTER NINE

SEPTEMBER 1939 — WORLD WAR II

I awoke with a start. March music interrupted by shouting voices and, drums beating, boomed from the radio. Despite the deafening noise, Mama just stood there. "Oh, Jesus, help us. We are at war," she said.

"Mama, what did you say?"

Before she could answer, the announcer's voice screamed excitedly, "We have been attacked! We have been attacked! Polish soldiers fired into our territory and since 4:45 a.m., our troops have returned the fire. Our Fuhrer vowed that he will put on his soldier coat and he will not take it off until victory is ours. We are at war!"

Mama held her bulging stomach. "I have never wanted to bring a baby into a war," she lamented. "Let us hope it is over soon."

"Mama, don't worry, our teacher said that our Fuhrer has taken Austria the Sudetenland back without firing a shot. He will find a way to settle this peacefully."

"This is Poland, not a German territory," Mama said.

She was right. On September 3, England, France, Australia, and New Zealand joined Poland and declared war on Germany. Even though the whole world was now against us, I believed that our Fuhrer told the truth when he promised that we would win World War II. While the weekly war reports at the movies brought us to the battlefield, and the radio announcers gave graphic details of the courageous battles our soldiers fought, at home everything remained much the same. For me, war was far away, in Poland, and we were going on with our lives until the first heroes of the war came home in plain wooden caskets. More young men were called to serve, small businesses closed, and several of Uncle Pepp's farm hands and bakery apprentices were drafted. When Uncle Pepp was ordered to increase production, he grumbled, "How do those bureaucrats think I can do that? My bakers work double shifts now."

Several days later, Karola, Resi and I heard men shouting at columns of ragged-looking men and women. We climbed the garden fence and watched while they hobbled past our home. The women's heads were covered by huge shawls or blankets, drab, loose dresses or skirts hid their bodies, some wore ill-fitting clodhoppers, and others walked barefooted. They followed several soldiers into the factory yard where they entered the barracks that had been built just a few weeks ago. We wondered where these people had come from and why they marched in columns to the factory.

Later that day, Uncle Pepp stopped by and told Mama, "The work placement office solved my labor shortage. Worm Sepp, all decked out in his SA uniform, stopped by and brought me labor workers from Poland: two men and two women. They don't speak a word of German, but we will have to manage. According to Sepp, the health department deloused every worker before they assigned them to work stations. Kasha, a young woman, barely seventeen, works in the kitchen, Maria will help Babette on the farm, and Roman and Wiedold start in the bakery."

After school, I asked Erna, "What do you think of the Poles?"

"So far they don't bother me." Erna said. "Come, and see for yourself." Kasha, her head cast downward, stood by the sink peeling potatoes. As she looked up, it was hard for me to hide my surprise. Unlike the ghost-like, ragged women I had seen, Kasha was beautiful. Her black curly hair framed her small face which gave her a sylph-like appearance, and her hazel eyes looked straight at me.

I pointed at her, "You are Kasha," I shouted, "and I Anneliese." I pointed at myself and repeated, "Anneliese."

"You don't have to shout," Erna said. "Kasha is not deaf. Give her time to listen. Repeating is fine, but don't burst her eardrums."

Within days, Uncle Pepp praised his labor workers. "They are quick learners, they already understand and speak a few German words, and they are good workers. Peppi, after Maria gets more familiar with the farm work, I can send Babette to help out when you are due."

Baby Irmgard joined our family on October 31, and she was almost three months old when Papa saw her for the first time.

Papa took me aside. "Anneliese," he said, "every Saturday morning, you will take English and typing lessons from the Sisters. You can handle the additional work, and I expect that you will do your best. The lessons are arranged and paid for."

"Papa," I protested, "why do I have to learn English? Our teacher said that we are going to win the war and then everybody will have to speak German. So why should I learn English? I know some Latin, isn't that enough?"

"Now you listen," Papa admonished. "You are going on fourteen, so you must start to plan for your future. Since we are at war, you can lose health, your home, or both. But people who know and have learned more than others are always needed. To make yourself proficient, you will need typing and English so learn all I offer you, and you will have a better life than we do."

The next morning, Karola waited for me at the school entrance. Before I could tell her what Papa had said, she cried out, "Anneliese, I don't know if I can go in there."

"What did you do?"

"It is not what I did. It is Mama. Can you believe it, she was arrested yesterday. Papa got her out of jail last night, but she will have to go to court in Weiden."

"Why would she be arrested?"

"Papa said that several witnesses accused Mama of slandering Mister Sommer, the high officials of the party, and their entourage. Last spring, way before the war, Mama was in the Market Square grocery store while the funeral procession of Councilor Sommer passed by. As the official party members, the SA, the standard banner carriers, groups of flag bearers and the BDM, (Union of German Girls) marched by, Mama said, 'Here come the party members' marriageable daughters in their shit brown uniforms. That's all they are, shit! I should unload some more on them . . . at least they wear the right color.' Then Mama went right past everyone, and she didn't even stop and salute the flags. Papa asked the chief why they waited so long to arrest her. The chief declared, 'We are now at war, and people like your wife are considered very dangerous since her remarks could undermine the morale and confidence of the people. The trial will be held on April 19, the day before the Fuhrer's birthday.' Oh, Anneliese, I wish I were dead."

I tried to reassure her. "It won't be so bad."

"It will be in all the county newspapers today, and it will also be hung out on the towns' bulletin boards." Karola cried out, "Just imagine how the Jung Maidens will tease me, and everyone in town will know. Oh, why do I have a mother like that?"

Everyone was talking about the upcoming trial. "She can think what she wants — but to say it?" Uncle Pepp said.

On April 19, Karola was not in school. Marerl and I wondered where Karola would live if they took her Mama. Her papa was a traveling salesman and he was away from home except for weekends and holidays. The trial was front page news. At a special court session, four witnesses testified that Karola's mama had publicly maligned the flag and the party.

The police chief testified, "Anna Siller has never been arrested before. She almost always speaks without thinking and she is known for that. I don't think the likes of her can shake the faith in our Fuhrer or the party within anyone. The Sommer family said that they won't ever pay attention to Mrs. Siller or people like her."

Since they were poor, the judge just warned her. "Mrs. Siller, if you come before me again, you will pay a large monetary fine, and then I will send you to the toughest prison to stay until you rot! Is that clear?"

"Yes, your Honor," she answered.

Karola recalled, "Mama came home that very night, ranting, 'Those wailing witnesses tried to dig me into prison to make themselves look good.' But Papa told her, 'Anna, it was all your fault, and if you do that again, I will leave you.' Papa is right, it is Mama's fault that people talk about us. It is all her fault."

We reminded Karola that within a few weeks people would find someone else to talk about, and they did. It was Max, my little brother, who became the talk of the town.

Mama had waited until Baby Irmgard was asleep. "Anneliese," she said, "I must take care of some errands. Resi will be with her friends, but you must watch Irmgard while I'm gone. Mrs. Lang will watch Max since he and her little Joseph play for hours with wooden remnants at the lumbermill."

Irmgard was sleeping peacefully, and a teen mystery book held my attention, until, suddenly, the shrillness of the fire whistle shattered my world of make-believe. The window was slightly ajar, and horrified, I looked at the pitch-black smoke billowing upward until it hid the blue sky and polluted the spring air. Barely two blocks away from our home, the lumbermill was now encircled by a reddish-golden wall of fire that spewed burning embers upward; dancing in the air, they splintered into glowing red cinder flakes and fell back to the ground. I stood numb with fear as firemen and the fire wagon raced toward the huge monster fire.

"Oh God, Max and Josef are at the lumbermill," I cried out. My hands shook as I picked up Irmgard, wrapped her in a blanket and ran into the garden. Just then Mama ran along the potato field and disappeared into the Lang house. The patrolmen shouted commands, horses whinnied, wheels of the fire wagons ground the gravel, and the fire bell competed with the noise of the fire wind, while the crowd inched back.

Fearfully, I searched the crowd and bolted forward as I spotted Mama and Max. "Thank God, you are safe." I held him and stroked his soot-covered hair.

Mama interrupted. "The fire is still raging. It will have to burn itself out. Anneliese, take Max inside, and don't bother him with questions."

His hair black from soot, and his eyes saucer-like, little Max was dazed and quiet. Just then the doorbell rang. The police chief and his deputy stood at the garden gate. "Anneliese, we must speak with your mama and little Max," the chief called out.

"Mama isn't here. She is trying to get in touch with Papa."

"We'll be back after we've interviewed the Langs," the chief said as they left.

Mama returned with Uncle Pepp and Grandma. "Peppi," Uncle Pepp said, "the police should be here shortly, and if you want, I'll speak for you. I should be able to do that since you weren't here while all of this took place."

Mama's eyes were red. "Pepp, that may be best. I truly thought the children were taken care of in my absence," she sighed.

Max clung tightly to Mama as the police chief entered and turned toward Max. "You don't have to be afraid, just answer my

questions. I don't lock little children up, and I don't hurt them."
Gently he went on, "Did you and Josef play in the lumbermill today?"

Max barely nodded.

"What did you play with?" the chief asked.

"Josef's little rabbits . . . They were cold , so we put . . . wood
blocks around them."

"And then," the chief coaxed.

"We wanted to keep the little rabbits warm, so we got matches
and built a fire. and the fire got so big. We grabbed the rabbits, but .
. . one . . . one got away, and we ran away too." Max shuddered. "Josef
and I ran to his house and we hid with the rabbits in his room. We
thought the fire would stop," Max sobbed.

The chief looked at Mama and Uncle Pepp. He nodded,
"Josef tells the same story. As far as I know, there won't be any
official action against the boys. What do you do with five-year-old
boys who want to keep rabbits warm?" He turned toward Max, "I
hope you won't ever play with matches again. You saw the big fire
they made. Now listen to your mama and papa when they tell you that
you must not play with matches."

Max kept nodding his head, long after the chief had turned
from him. For days after the fire, I wished Max was not my brother
because then people wouldn't look at me and say, "Her brother and
the Lang boy started the mill fire."

Mama said that I just should ignore these remarks, but that
was not so easy. During recess, Mary came up to me. "You think you
are so smart and special, but I tell you, you are not! My mama said
that if your papa were home, like my papa, he could pay attention to
Max. Your mama wasn't even home when Max ran around and burnt
the mill. Somebody should be in jail!"

Hanni, who stood next to Mary, broke in. "She is right! Your
papa and mama think they are so special, too. They don't join the
Party, and they don't let you join the Young Maidens. My mama's
friends have to volunteer for double shifts at the mill, just because
your papa isn't home to take care of Max, and your mama can't take
even care of you. What are you doing for the war effort now that your
brother has stopped work at the mill?"

"Come," Mary hissed. "Let's not waste our time on her. The
Solchs, except for Hans, are all alike."

I stood thunderstruck. I had thought Mary was nicer than her sister Rosa. No one liked me or my family, and it was all Max's fault.

"That's people," Karola consoled. "My mama always says, 'People talk about somebody else, so they can feel better.'"

Uncle Pepp was talking with Mama when I came home. "I wish I was back in the Witness School," I cried out. "At least everyone was nice there." Before Mama could ask, I told of the morning confrontation that had exposed me to my classmates feelings. "I didn't know they hate me that much, and Mama, they don't like you, they don't like Papa, and they don't like Uncle Pepp, either," I cried out.

"Anneliese, that's why I am here with your mama," Uncle Pepp said. " I heard talk too and we can't do anything about it. The war has everyone on edge, and people say things they wouldn't say otherwise. You hold your head up high, and be proud of your whole family. Remember, there always have been and there always will be people who are jealous and mean-spirited. We won't stoop to their level. Stay away from them."

"That's easy for you to say. Rosa's sister sits two rows ahead of me, and her friends are all around me."

"Nevertheless, I say, avoid her and her friends. Don't give them the satisfaction that you are hurt by their remarks. The sooner you learn that, the better off you will be."

Mama hugged me. "Pepp is right, Anneliese, our whole family is learning more than I ever wanted to know. Spring break should help you."

CHAPTER TEN

THE WAR EXPANDS AND HOME FRONT
EFFORTS INTENSIFY

The 1940 Spring Break ended, I was going on fourteen, and we started eighth grade. On a wall map, we followed our forces to the expanding fronts, and our teacher encouraged us to pin the Norwegian towns they had conquered. Norway, on our huge European map, was covered with miniature Swastika flags, and on May 10, the big offensive against the Western Front began. During May and into June, our daily school reports followed the retreat of the French soldiers until their surrender.

"The British at Dunkirk are involved in a life-and-death struggle," our teacher lectured. "We will push them into the sea. That should give them a warning and if they don't heed it, we will show them what we can do."

We cheered as the newsreels showed the French General Huntziger signing the armistice with Germany in the Compiegne Railway Carriage where the 1918 humiliation of Germany had taken place. We were with Mama's brother, Uncle Anton, and his wife, Aunt Lore, and Cousin Alfred. As always, Uncle Anton put his crutches aside and he took us back to 1918 when he had fought at Somme, in France. "We didn't have the modern weapons of today, but I think our weapons were equally gruesome. Not only was it always foggy and muddy there, the enemy was often face-to-face as well. During a fierce battle, an artillery shell took my right leg right off from the crotch, but the gas --- the poisonous gas was so overpowering that even my gas mask didn't help. My lungs burnt and they were so severely damaged, that I can't take a deep breath to this day." He turned toward Mama and Aunt Lore. "It makes me feel good to see Adolf Hitler avenge the humiliation of Germany. Now, we are on their turf. Let them feel the humiliation and defeat, let's see how they like it!" he said.

"Anton, what good will all that glory do?" Aunt Lori interrupted. "Just wait, it won't be long and they will take Alfred. Do you want our son to go through what we have lived with? World War I has been over for twenty-two years, and yet, it dominates our life every day — every day! Now we can watch Alfred go through the same hell you did. Well, I say keep your glory and let our son stay well and safe! That's all I want."

The room was still. Aunt Lore's apron went toward her face as she left the room while Mama responded, "Anton, you are still fighting the First World War. Now we are in the Second, and nothing has changed — soldiers on both sides still maim and kill."

Little Max, who had listened and was captivated by Uncle Anton's story, pointed his index finger at us and said, "When I get big, I'll go to war and I fight and shoot. POW, pow, pow! Pow! Everyone is dead."

During the summer the war expanded. We flocked to the movie theater, and watched our Stuka planes penetrating the skies over London, Sheffield, Liverpool, and other British cities. As their deadly loads of bombs exploded, buildings burnt and crumbled like paper. Italy, our ally, was fighting in North Africa and Greece , while our U-boats and tankers crisscrossed the seas in search of targets. At the movies, we could feel close to our fighting forces, as we cheered their victories and the blazing glory of war.

To assure unity at home, listening to foreign radio broadcasts became a crime, and punishment for the first offense was five to ten years in a prison for political dissidents. Right after Christmas Adolf Hitler mandated that fourteen and fifteen-year-old girls must complete the Pflichtjahr, a year of duty, working either for a family with at least four children under the age of twelve, working at a farmstead or a business place connected to the war effort. School attendance for Pflichtjahr students was cut to one day.

Competing with other mothers, Mama was happy when Mrs. Pach told her, "Anneliese may work for us. Although our maid will do the heavy work, Anneliese must start at 6:30 a.m. and work until 8:00 p.m., except on Saturdays it will be later since the grocery store and the storage rooms are scrubbed also. She won't have to work on Sundays and Monday afternoons, but otherwise her time is ours. We pay the wage scale, fifteen marks a month."

"Anneliese, I suggest you work for the Pachs." Mama urged. "You can stay at home, and a year is not forever. Since you work, there won't be time for English lessons. I imagine you are sad about that." Marerl was elated. "I'm scheduled to start at a restaurant," she told me. "Can you believe it, the work commissioner placed Karola on a farm. We must attend a placement meeting where we'll get our rules and hear why we must leave school and why we must go to work."

"You, our young people, are our future," the commissioner told us. "Since our soldiers protect you and give their lives, it is important that you become responsible workers who don't quit! If you do, I will find you a new place to work and you will start anew." He smiled. "Now that would not be very smart, would it? Just ask the girl who has worked for two years now, and she is on the third month of her year of duty. I think she's finally learned that 'Workers never quit!' It is our duty to prepare you so you will learn to love work and duty."

My year of duty was a time of rude awakening. I realized living at home had been a fourteen-year vacation because, within days, I learned that I could rarely think of my wants or needs. After I arrived at the Pach's at 6:30 a.m., Mrs. Pach introduced me to her family, and she handed me a sheet with my weekly duties clearly stated. Mondays was washday, and the rest of the week was taken up with ironing, patching, and general housework. But the care for three spoiled, whining preschoolers was my main responsibility.

"Mama, I will never last," I complained after an especially trying day.

"Anneliese, you will try — and not just for a week or two because we are not known as quitters," she said. "Everyone is expected to work more since our men are on the front so do your best. Hard work won't hurt you, and you will survive the year. I don't want to hear any more complaints."

There was no way out, so reluctantly I went back and endured Mrs. Pach's unreasonable demands. She enjoyed finding scouring powder that I couldn't see on silverware, or dust that she imagined lurking in corners. After she duly reprimanded Mathilde or me for our shortcomings, we had to re-wash or dust all over again so we would learn to do our work right the first time.

Resi, my classmate, was next door at the tailor's household. On Monday, on the way to school, we compared our lot. She heard me out, then anguished, "You think you have it tough? You have a maid to do the heavy work. How would you like to be stuck with six snot-nosed girls, all day long? Let me tell you, Anneliese, there is nothing better than being an only child. Our Fuhrer can advocate marriage to the Young Maidens, but I will never get married, and no one will ever convince me to have children. When I complained to Papa, he said, 'I hear you. It is settled. If you stay single, you must become a nun.'"

Marerl and Karola hadn't fared much better. Marerl washed restaurant dishes after meals and then, late into the night, she scrubbed tables and floors until her bones ached and dead tired, she fell into bed. Karola worked on the farm. Since Mister Grarl had been drafted, Mrs. Grarl and Karola shared men's work and she adapted quickly.

"You should have seen me when I directed the ox team for the first time. Now, I turn the hay and bring home a load of fodder. Can you believe it? Since the vegetable garden is in my care, there isn't a weed standing." She showed us the blisters on her hands, and her sunburnt arms and legs. "I will never marry a farmer," she vowed. "All they have on their mind is work, work, work, and then they remember work that should have been done last winter."

Suddenly everyone loved school, and Monday's afternoon classes had perfect attendance. At least we could share how we fared, and we could console each other. It seemed our own work situation was almost always better than someone else's. We took solace in the thought that every Monday we met, we were closer to the completion of our year of duty. Our teacher reminded us that a year ago, on June 22, France had signed the armistice agreement with Germany, and she encouraged us to write to our soldiers on distant fronts.

CHAPTER ELEVEN

THE RUSSIAN FRONT

June 22, 1941 was a beautiful day, but the cloudless sky belied what was taking place on the borders of Russia. I was at work when Mrs. Pach walked into the kitchen,

"When will it ever end?" she said. "Now, just now, I heard on the radio that our Fuhrer has broken the Non-Aggression Pact we had with Russia, and our soldiers are fighting on Russian ground since early this morning. We may as well prepare for the worst."

We heard and we watched as the newsreels showed again how rapidly our soldiers advanced deeply into Russia under the slogan, 'Nothing is impossible for the German soldier as long as you, at home, increase your effort and support.'

Men, who until now had felt they were draft-exempt, received their notices, and women were placed in their work positions. The fighting on the East Front intensified. During Monday's class, we listened and learned of the suffering war inflicted families at home.

Maria Beer stood up and shared how her family coped. "Mama and Papa have five sons serving the Fatherland. Three of my brothers are on the fronts, fighting: Max, the oldest, is with a tank unit spearheading into Russia and paving the way into Stalingrad. He was to come home on furlough after the fighting in France, but he never did. Josef, barely nineteen, is an officer's driver. The last we heard, they were advancing — their final destination is Moscow." Maria sighed and went on. "So far, Franz is lucky. He is still in France, part of the occupational force. Martin, eighteen, was drafted last week, and Otto, who is seventeen, has his number and is in training. Mama fears that soon they, too, will be on the front. Herman is fourteen now, and Mama hopes that the war will be over before he is seventeen. Herman already says he wants to follow his brothers."

We joined our teacher as she applauded the courage and reiterated the fear and pain Maria's family endured. After school, several of us walked with Maria and asked her to tell us more.

"Every evening," she said, "nine-year-old Rosa, seven-year-old Ludmilla, little Adolf, who is six, and I kneel with Mama and pray for my brothers. We kneel in the four corners of Mama's bedroom so we can cover East, West, North and South. First, we pray the rosary, and then we ask God to have the guardian angels spread their wings around our brothers. Before we pray for us, we say the Lord's Prayer for all our soldiers. I know Mama doesn't sleep much. She has so much work since she prepares meals for the family and the workers. The foreign workers keep the farm and the machine shop going while my brothers invade and fight in their homelands. Papa says that the war is eating Mama's insides. Almost every night, Mama holds little Adolf, rocks him and laments, 'I had fifteen children. Three died, and five are on the front. You, little Adolf, were our seventh boy. We knew that Adolf Hitler would be your godfather; and you, too, will be taken from me on your tenth birthday. It is law.'"

Maria paused. "Why will little Adolf leave us?' I asked Mama. Tears lodged in Mama's wrinkles, as she went on, 'Maria, Adolf Hitler decreed that he will be the godfather of every seventh boy born into a family. Each godchild receives a fifty mark savings bond, and with average grades is fated to attend the Adolf Hitler school in Munich. I pray little Adolf can stay home.' I wonder how much more Mama can take?" Maria pondered.

Draft notices multiplied. Cousin Hans was drafted, and Aunt Lore and Uncle Anton knew that Cousin Alfred was front bound.

As Christmas 1941 neared, the whole world was enmeshed in war. On December 7, Japan bombed Pearl Harbor and completed air raids in Guam, Wake Island and Midway. America had entered the war. All this prompted my essay.

THE WAR IS NOT ONLY A DESTROYER, IT IS ALSO A DISCIPLINARIAN

Through the war politics of the English government the clouds of war constricted over our national, socialistic Germany. While Adolf Hitler frequently offered his hands to find peaceful solutions, the hate mongers in England and France refused to work on a covenant for peace. Polish soldiers frequently assaulted helpless German women, children and the elderly. When these violations did not cease, Germany declared war on Poland. England and France also became our declared enemies. By now, our enemies must realize that they are not dealing with the Germany of 1918!

Surely, WAR IS A DESTROYER, BUT IT IS ALSO A DISCIPLINARIAN. It destroys the happiness of families, since war takes away husbands, and fathers and sons. Some of these brave men will never return, because the war tore them from their comrades' sides as they fought. At home, the German wife and mother courageously carries the cruel blows of war. She knows that the whole German nation stands behind her and helps as she carries the burden. But these losses will not make us weaker, they will fuse us together as one. During peacetime some people lived for enjoyment and thought only of themselves. Now, during these difficult times, they are required to take on responsibilities and forego their former, carefree life styles. We must deny the longing for things we would like to have and go without. Every individual must obey the black-out law since even the thinnest dot or line of light could show the enemy bombers the targets they seek and cause loss of lives and homes. So through working together as a nation, we can work toward victory and peace. God blesses a nation which loves to work and serves the peace.

Spring 1942 had arrived and we were relieved. Since our year of duty neared completion, we had to secure other employment. Marerl secured work as a dress maker's apprentice. Karola and I applied for kindergarten internship. Karola was hired by the local kindergarten, and I waited for placement at Coburg, fifty miles from home.

The program leader told me, "It may be a few weeks before you will be placed where apprentices are needed most. Presently, all available trains are used for the children's evacuation."

CHAPTER TWELVE

CHILDREN'S EVACUATION

After 1940, Hamburg, Berlin and other metropolitan areas experienced frequent, saturation bombing. In 1942, our Fuhrer ordered parents within target cities, "Prepare your children, four through fourteen, for evacuation. We must protect them and save their lives."

Among other cities, Cologne had endured one nightly bombing where 1,000 bombers darkened and then lit up the night sky. The bombers' deadly cargo had left 45,000 homeless and the evacuation of children had become a weekly event. While the target cities became childless, our town received seventy-five tired and apprehensive young evacuees. Their leader walked alongside until they entered the Hitler Youth Home.

During the welcome ceremony, Mister Schmidt, the director, stood at the podium and told the listeners, "For weeks, thousands of train coaches, buses and steamboats have transported our children and brought them to safe havens in the Sudetenland, Thuringa, Austria, and Bavaria. These courageous young people left their mothers and fathers, sisters and brothers, so my assistant and I are their substitute family heads. All throughout Germany, students like these are placed in camps or public halls, but after six to eight months our groups are rotated to another area. We believe we will be happy here, so please come and visit us on weekends."

Uncle Pepp did go and visit, and the director told him, "Not every camp is equipped like this one. I don't agree with the rotation policy, because every change is upsetting for the already frayed emotions of these students. But no one asked us! My students have to cope with unimaginable stresses, they suffer from homesickness, loss of their family during air raids, then they worry about their fathers and brothers on the front. Several of my students have become orphans since we left Hamburg. I was a fifth grade teacher when the education department gave me this assignment which is the hardest, most heartbreaking job I ever had. There are benefits, though, I won't get drafted, and I don't have to spend nights in the basement being bombed."

Mama was not pleased when I told her that I had met the director's assistant, seventeen-year-old Hans Treich who had been wounded in a bombing. What drew me to him was the fact that he was an atheist. So far, I had never met an atheist so I wanted to know what atheists believed. Hans said there was no God, the sun controlled day, night, the earth and all that was in it because without the sun we would be plunged into darkness, choke and freeze to death.

"Who created the sun for you?" I asked him. "It was my God who was always there, and he created the sun, the earth, and everything in it!"

"Well," he retorted, "you say your God was always there, so why can't I say the same about the sun?"

I wanted to learn more, and talk with him about being a Catholic, but Mama said that would not happen because I had been granted admission to the kindergarten school in Coburg. Since I was not yet sixteen, a three-month trial period was prerequisite.

I loved being with the children, and shortly before I completed my twelve weeks the supervisor informed me, "Anneliese, your leader and I are pleased with your work. You may work here until school starts in January, but there is one thing you must do at once. We found you are not registered as a Nazi Party member. Since you must register in your home town, take several vacation days and return as a registered Nazi Party member. We can not send you on to school without your registration number."

I was happy and proud. I couldn't wait to tell Mama and Papa, but Papa reacted sternly. "Anneliese, you will not start at the school," he said.

"But Papa," I pleaded, "I need to register at the Nazi Party. Please, Papa, I don't know why you had never let me join Hitler's Young Maidens before, but now, I must become a member because that is the only way I can go on to school and become a teacher. You know I always wanted to be a teacher."

Papa stood firm. "No, Anneliese, I will find other work for you. You must tell your supervisor you will start in a war-effort position, most likely at the post office. Come home, and I will arrange the rest."

It didn't matter that I was furious. All my life Papa had told me what to do, and now he as telling me again. Just for once, I wish he would tell me why I could not join the Nazi Party when almost everyone I knew belonged. Why wouldn't he let me choose? When I was young I wanted to join the Young Maidens because I wanted the uniform and belong with my friends, but now I was older and I needed to join because all I wanted to be now — was a teacher.

CHAPTER THIRTEEN

JANUARY 1943 — REGENSBURG

As Papa had promised, he contacted Postmaster Roth who interviewed me briefly, and immediately placed me in the next postal employment testing. Two weeks later Mr. Roth told me that I had an almost perfect score in geography, so the district office classified me as a telegraph apprentice and gave me immediate employment at the Regensburg office.

Now I stood in the depot with Mama, Resi, Max, and Baby Irmgard, and Mama, again, voiced her concerns. "Anneliese, remember you are barely sixteen. Think before you act, and remember what we have taught you."

"Mama, don't worry, I will be all right."

She sighed. "You should be all right, since the postmaster and I arranged your lodging with the Sisters of St. Augustin's boarding school, yet, I won't rest until I know how you fare."

The final boarding call stopped Mama's instructions and shortened our good-byes. After a slow start, the old black engine smoothly pulled the five coaches through four miles of forest to the Wiesau railroad center. From my window seat I watched the patterns of deer footprints as they broke long stretches of the white, glistening snow blanket, and an unseen animal disturbed the birds as they scurried away from the branches of evergreens. After a brief stop, the train wound its way past Weiden, on to the ancient city of Nabburg built high on a hill. Hundreds of years ago, high walls a foot thick, protected the city from foreign intruders, but now these walls secluded residents from curious onlookers.

The conductor called out, "Schwandorf . . . next stop Regensburg!"

My heart pounded wildly. Long before the train slowed down on its approach, the spires of the cathedral greeted us. Papa had told me, "You will love the city. Regensburg has historic sites dating back to 200 A.D." Whenever I asked Papa about the cities he worked in, he would say, "Come, we will find it on the map because you must always know the way to where you are going, and the you must be able to find your way back." Then I would learn about the city near his work, the surrounding cities, rivers and famous sights. I know that his geography games were the reason for my high score and my work placement.

At the orientation at the telegraph office, I met four new apprentices, and I was paired off with Emma, who came from Waldsassen. She was taller than I and, while I was blond and fair, she had raven-black hair which she combed straight back from her forehead. We differed when it came to religion, music and food, but at work we rooted for each other during quizzes and tests.

After eight weeks, our supervisor lectured. "You passed your tests, and now you are ready to work on your own, so remember your heavy responsibilities. All civilian cables must be sent efficiently. However, one wrong letter on a coded military cable or a business shipment can spell disaster for you — and our office. We are known for speed and accuracy, and I expect you will not diminish our performance. Never leave your work station until your replacement has signed in. If you have doubts about a procedure, ask. Now let us work."

Within weeks I was acclimated to the intensive and challenging work, but I was desperately unhappy living at Saint Augustine's boarding school. Since the Sisters had taken in more students than the boarding house could handle, my dorm room was a damp, closet-size basement room.

When sinus headaches disrupted my sleep, I wrote to Mama, "My deplorable lodging situation is affecting my health and my work. Please, try to help me."

"No," Mama wrote back. "It is time you handle your own problems. Talk with your supervisor."

My supervisor listened politely and located new lodging. My own room! I thought, but it wasn't. My new landlady gave her rowdy friends permission to use and sleep in my room while I was at work.

Their secondhand smoke, soiled clothing, and my used bed sheets left me frustrated and angry.

I returned to the telegraph office and complained. The supervisor shook his head, "Miss Solch, I believe that things can be bad once, but two landlords — I don't know how the housing department will view this."

"Please," I pleaded, "come with me and you will see I'm telling you the truth."

"That's what we get when we have to hire students barely out of school. I don't have enough problems? Now, I have to play being their father," he muttered.

The next day he stopped by my work station and said, "Miss Solch, tonight after work you will be moving. I saw your landlady and while I was there two couples used your room, so we blacklisted her — we won't rent from her again. The Lehnerts expect you tonight. You may have seen or heard of Luther Lehnert, the head baritone at the Regensburg Opera. If you like opera or at least pretend you do, you should be fine."

I didn't have to worry. I felt instantly drawn to the tall, slim woman as she came toward me and her long, slim fingers of both hands clasped my hands firmly.

"I am Hannah Lehnert," she said, "and this is Luther, my husband. We are so glad to have you. The housing authority just advised us that we had a choice: we were to relinquish a bedroom to bombing victims from Lubeck or Cologne or to someone who worked in a war-effort industry. I think we made the right choice. It will be good for us, too, having a young lady living here."

She led me toward on open door. "As you can see, your room is sparsely furnished but the bed and the down covers are clean and comfortable. You may add your own items as you wish, and you may also join us in the living room whenever you like. Luther completes most of his rehearsing and warmups at the opera house. You should know though, there are times when he brings his work home. Do you like opera?"

"Yes, I do," I assured them. I tried to remain calm, but I felt euphoric . . . this was my second home, and I didn't ever want to lose it. Now that my housing worries were over, I worked intensely honing my skills while Mrs. Lehnert opened up a new world for me.

She encouraged me to use the books from their extensive collection, she invited me to attend operas and symphonies with her, and she never tired of answering my questions. Whenever I walked into their living room, I could shut out work and the war.

Despite the defeat at Stalingrad, our Fuhrer threatened that our soldiers would crush the Russian Army during the summer campaign. During March, our U-Boats had sunk seventy-four British freighters and tankers. Mothers and wives were worried at home because their husbands and sons fought daily battles in foreign lands. When we talked at work, we talked of the time when our soldiers would bring the war to a victorious end. Although the war dominated the quality of living conditions and standards, we tried to maintain a certain degree of normalcy.

Emma told me one day, "Anneliese, my rooming situation is similar to what you encountered. I am moving out and my new quarters will be near yours."

Since we were assigned to the same shifts, we met and walked through the park which led to the Thurn-and-Taxis castle. Secluded behind those high walls, high towers, and crowns of trees, lived a real prince, the Prince of Thurn-and-Taxis. A shortcut through historic Cow Street, barely three feet wide, led us past the cathedral. Right across from it was the entrance to the telegraph building. When we had split shifts, we took the trolley and explored the Old Town, where century old buildings bound the shores of the Blue Danube, foreign laborers worked on boats, and sailors walked in and out of the Red Light streets. We learned much about each other during our walks.

When I told Emma that I was reading about and listening to the music of our classical composers, she replied, "I'm glad I don't live there. All this opera stuff makes me sick. Our modern composers do much better. Come to the Dome Kaffee with me, and you'll see."

The winter had passed, and we were enjoying the beautiful spring days of 1943 when one of Emma's co-workers approached me. "Anneliese, you are Emma's friend. Have you noticed the sudden rashes that come and go on Emma's skin? We wondered if she has something contagious, so Heidi asked her to see the company nurse, but we know she hasn't. Tell her, tonight, we won't tolerate this much longer. If she is sick, she should go to a doctor and not expose us to her illness."

On our way home I asked Emma, "Are you ill?"

"I have been waiting for you to say something, but you are always so busy with the Lehnerts that you don't even know what is going on around you," she reproached. "Yes, I am sick, and I don't know what to do about it because it involves other people too."

"Do you have . . . something contagious, like measles?"

"Yes, . . . and no . . . but it is worse than you think."

"It can't be that bad. You are up and working."

"That's what I mean. You think you are so smart, but you don't know anything," she snapped.

"Well, then, enlighten me!" I said.

We sat down on a park bench. After a moment, Emma haltingly began, "I have met someone . . . a man."

Surprised, I repeated, "A man? So how can that make you sick?"

I was startled by the anger in her eyes. "Sometimes, you are...oh, forget it. Anyway, you would not approve of the man I met ...nor would any one else. But I love him, oh, God, I love him! I can not imagine life without him." Tears streamed down her face as she pleaded, "Swear you won't tell anyone."

"I won't ever tell," I promised somberly.

She looked around and then went on. "The man is a foreign labor worker from France. I won't give you his name. If they ever suspected anything, and you were questioned, you couldn't name him."

"Emma, how can you take such a chance? You know the punishment. You are a telegraph worker and you work with coded Armed Forces information coming over the wires every day. Have you lost your mind?"

"I would never divulge information to anyone. We are not interested in the Army's secret information, and I am not crazy, but I may be soon."

"What do you mean?"

"I don't know how to tell you any other way: I have slept with him, not at first, but we have slept together for several months now."

"Months? Months? Why didn't I see you with him?"

"Because we are very careful and secretive. We meet after his nightly bed check. Whenever his buddies can cover for him, he sneaks past the guards, out of the camp, and then he walks past my window until I can let him in. Since my landlady is old and hard of hearing, she never knows whether I am working or in my room. We meet whenever and wherever we can. Passersby have never bothered us. They must think I am French, too."

"Emma, you are beautiful, and I thought you were smart, too. But — you are crazy! You are risking your life for a foreign labor worker? I swear, I would die before I get involved with a foreign worker."

"How can you say that? Why should it make any difference where we were born? Neither he, I, nor you had any control over that. Anneliese, when I am with him, we are not German and French, and we are not enemies — we are a man and a woman in love."

"Oh, yes, when you are caught, the judge will be delighted to hear that! You will be imprisoned or, worse yet, you could be sentenced to death."

"I may be dead, already. You asked me about my rash, if it was measles. It isn't. My rash is far more serious."

"How do you know?"

"Pierre told me." Her hand cupped her mouth, and her eyes widened in realization . . . "Now you know his name, but please, forget it, forever. Anyway, he told me that he never knew he had syphilis in the early stages when he met me. Now that I am already infected, he will not ask for treatment because he would be shipped off to a hard labor camp, immediately. We hope the war ends soon. Then we can get treatment before the third stage starts."

"So in the meantime he infects you, and who knows how many other unsuspecting German girls?"

"That's not true, he is faithful to me, and he is careful, so that no one finds out. You must remember, Pierre was a victim too. His father owns several banks in France, Pierre attended the best schools, he speaks fluent German, and now he is reduced to a laborer. Despite all this, he is not out for vengeance because he is good and kind. You don't know him, but I do. No matter what you say, we will stay together because we love each other. I know you can't understand, but it doesn't matter, I will always love him."

"No," I interjected, "I will never understand how anyone can love a foreigner, an enemy yet, but my understanding or approval doesn't matter. You must go to a doctor and get treatment. Do at least that much for yourself and for me. If you don't, your coworkers will turn you in to the supervisor and then you will have no choice. Think of the consequences. Let me tell them you are seeing a doctor."

"What will I tell the good doctor? 'Doctor, I'm sleeping with a foreign labor worker and he gave me syphilis, so please cure me and him, too.' You know what will happen? He will have to report us, and we'll be shipped off to prison or to make an example of associating with the enemy, we must die. I would sooner be with him until we both die of syphilis."

"You can't do that! I'll ask Mister Lehnert for advice without giving your name. I know he won't tell anyone because for him, a promise is a promise."

"I don't care about myself, but I love him so," Emma went on. "If it wasn't for the war, we would not be in this situation. Go ahead and talk with Mister Lehnert, and we can see if he has a solution."

Mr. Lehnert reacted like I thought he would. "Indeed," he said, "your co-worker should contact Dr. Kohl and tell him the following: 'Some time ago I spent several nights with a sergeant home on furlough from France. I found out later that he gave me a fictitious name and address and everything else he told me was a lie. All he left me with was syphilis.' I doubt Dr. Kohl will trace a fictitious name — he is too busy for that."

Emma was elated when she returned from her appointment. "It turned out exactly as Mister Lehnert had said it would. Dr. Kohl suggested that since he is unable to trace the sergeant who transmitted the disease, he will concentrate on keeping my infection in check. Since I am in the second stage of the disease, he injects me with heavy doses of penicillin which will eliminate the rash and, hopefully, keep the infection in check. He also insisted that I take condoms with me for partners' protection. I am not sure if he believed my story."

Despite the risks, Emma met Pierre whenever she could. One evening we were on our way home when two French-speaking men passed us and then kept pace with us.

"The one on the right is Pierre. We are meeting tonight," Emma said.

Dumbfounded I asked, "How do you know that?"

"He nodded his head twice, but, for our protection, he never uses the same signal again. Now you have seen him. I hope you're satisfied."

"Sure, I saw his back. What a wonderful back he has." We laughed and I went on my way.

Since our work hours had been increased to "as need arises," our days off had been sharply curtailed. "Tomorrow, Anita will trade shifts with me," I told Emma. If I take the evening train home, I'll be in Wiesau around midnight, and then I will have a whole day at home."

"You'll sleep in the waiting room in Wiesau until morning?"

"No, I take the four mile shortcut through the woods, and in an hour I will be home sleeping in my own bed," I said.

"What does your mama say to that?"

"I haven't told her. When I ring the bell, she will be so happy to see me. I don't think she'll be angry, not for long anyway."

After an uneventful train ride, I arrived in Wiesau at midnight. I waited until all departing passengers went on their way, and then I walked alongside the railroad tracks until Wiesau lay behind me. Total blackout enveloped the countryside in pitch-blackness, and its open spaces looked boundless. The low-hanging night clouds seemed to touch the tips of the tall fir trees, the leaves of underbrush rustled in the wind, and the sounds of nocturnal creatures around me kept me tense and watchful. Whenever I reached a clearing, and outlines of small farm homes broke the spread of fields, I looked straight ahead and ran until the safety of the dark woods took me in once more. Finally, the woods became sparse, and the trail led past the foreign labor workers' barracks which had been shut down for the night. As I neared the buildings, fear gripped me. I didn't know these people who came from foreign lands, it was dark, and no one at home expected me. If workers saw me, would they harm me? I prayed to God to keep my guardian angel by my side and grant me safe passage. Then I thought of Uncle Pepp's foreign workers, Kasha and Wiedold, and I felt better. Their demeanor had convinced me that they would never harm anyone. Still apprehensive, I cautiously took the long way around the site and finally, I reached our garden gate. I leaned on the gate and rang the bell.

"Mama," I called out, "let me in."

She met me in the foyer and hugged me. "Anneliese, it is past midnight, how did you get home?"

"I came on the train and walked home from Wiesau."

"Alone?"

"Yes."

"How could you, Anneliese?"

"I didn't have time to wait until morning. I wanted to be home with you."

Fatigue, fear, and all the uncertainties which I had pushed back welled up and I felt drained. I looked around, and I was startled by the changes I saw. Max was sleeping on the sofa in the kitchen.

"Is Max sick?" I asked.

"He is not sick. Since you left, much has happened. I wrote Papa, so he knows about the changes, but I thought I wouldn't worry you until everything was settled. Tomorrow, you will meet our renters."

"You're talking about renters? When did we get renters?" I asked.

"Pepp advised me to rent the upper rooms while I still could choose who would live here. He brought Erna, and while we sorted and cleaned, his labor workers moved the furniture into place. I don't know what we would have done without their help. Since the enemy air raids increased, thousands of people are homeless, so as of now, a housing official determines with whom and with how many homeless we must share our home. There is no choice, and no appeal. We were lucky, because our renters, the Dimpfls and their little boy and girl, are very nice people. We gave them furniture, bedding and whatever we could spare. Her folks are bombed out too and they live here for several weeks and then they live with their other daughter near Hof. For us, it could be worse: Irmgard sleeps in your bed, and Max sleeps on the sofa in the kitchen. We moved your bed and other furniture into the living room, and Resi sleeps in Max's room."

Mama shuddered. "We'll talk more in the morning. Thank God, you are safe, and now, we need rest."

I still tried to absorb all the changes that had taken place. "Come," Mama said, "I will show you your 'new' room, and then you must get rest."

I followed and walked into the bedroom-living room

Jewish families forcefully removed from their homes. They were allowed to take fifty small marks and one suitcase — to destinations unknown to them or their families.

combination. Irmgard was sleeping soundly in my bed. Mama picked her up, and without a word carried her into her bedroom.

Early the next morning after breakfast, Max and Irmgard rarely left me out of sight, and Mama said, "It is hard for the little ones to understand all these drastic changes within our living quarters. The war effort is becoming intense. Pepp spoke with the mayor; so far, our town has lost fifteen men on the Western Front, but Russia swallows our husbands and sons: during the past two years, 112 men have died." She thought for a moment. "Oh, yes, I meant to tell you earlier. Poor Mrs. Beer, Maria's mother, had five sons on the front. A month ago, twenty-two-year-old Josef died in Russia when a sharpshooter shot him in the head. Max, who had been wounded in Stalingrad, already has orders to return to his unit as soon as he is well. Hans and Alfred, your cousins, received their draft notices to the Grafenwoehr Army base." Mama shook her head. "Where will it end?"

Shock rippled through me. "Poor Maria. I won't be able to see her any time soon. Our supervisor said that we'll have to work harder — double shifts for Christmas — so I won't come home, but Papa will come home, won't he?"

"Yes, I am sure he will. We will miss you, but we feel better since we know you are with the Lehnerts."

"Mama, when I first moved there, Mrs. Lehnert didn't say much. But then, she told me that until a year ago, she had Jewish friends. Then last year during April, the SA picked a hundred Jewish men and women, marched them through the streets, and forcefully took them from Regensburg. She doesn't know where her friends are, or what they are doing."

"It's a good thing the Freiman family emigrated to America. I am glad they did. Mister Klein sold his store, and no one knows where he is."

After supper, my family came with me to the depot. I realized why it was so hard to leave. There were so many changes taking place, and we weren't part of each others' daily lives any longer. Pursuing other interests, even Karola and Marerl seemed to be drifting away.

CHAPTER FOURTEEN

BOMBING CASUALTIES

Between July 24 and August 2, the Hamburg telegraph connections were out of order. Radio announcers reported that all of Hamburg was an inferno and they graphically described how eight square miles of buildings had burned to the ground in the fire storms the American B-17 had unleashed. One said that hurricane winds, explosions, intense fires and lack of oxygen had driven people from the shelters on to the streets where hot, glue-like tar held them in a vice. By morning, after eight hours of inferno, more than 42,000 civilians had died, tens of thousands were injured, and 800,000 civilians were now homeless.

One of the Fuhrer's adjutants called for everyone outside Hamburg to open their homes to the bombing victims. Housing laws became even more restrictive, and all home- and apartment-owners outside Hamburg were ordered to make room for homeless families. Uncle Pepp's foresight had saved Mama from having undesirable renters in our home.

In Regensburg we saw the bombed-out homeless as they came with their few bundles. We listened to their stories of horror and we felt sorry for them, but within weeks they were present in such great numbers that we didn't take notice anymore. The massive bombings took their toll on every aspect of life; besides food and housing space, utilities and clothing were now also rationed.

At noon on August 17, with six hours of rush work already behind me, I longed for my break. Anita, who worked nearby in an office called. "Anneliese, I will have lunch with Papa at the Messerschmitt plant. It is one of these summer days where you just want to be outside, so come along."

Minutes later we boarded the trolley. After the trolley's first stop, I told Anita, "I hope you won't mind, but I will get off at the next stop and go back to the office."

Anita looked puzzled. "Why would you want to do that?"

I tried to explain. "There are things I left undone, and my replacement shouldn't have to worry about that."

"You eat, sleep and dream office," she laughed. "Get out of here."

I waved to her as I got off. Just as I closed the heavy door to the telegraph office, the shrill sound of the air raid siren shattered the calm of the cloudless summer day. In the shelter, Gisela volunteered and manned the information station where deadly silence held us captive while we listened. Hundreds of American bombers and a number of fighter planes were flying on to Schweinfurt, while more than a hundred planes changed course to Regensburg.

We sat numb with fear while Gisela recorded and relayed information: "Bombers over the Messerschmitt plant."

The sudden rumble of angry earth was disturbing; muffled sounds of explosions and the drone of low flying planes filled the shelter. Finally, the rumble and the noise subsided, and an hour later, we could return to work. Everyone who knew the whereabouts of Anita was even more concerned for her safety after our supervisor heard about the destruction within the Messerschmitt plant. The area was "off limits" except for ambulances, fire engines, soldiers and other support personnel. There was nothing for me to do but to go home and wait.

Two days had passed, and I couldn't concentrate at work because Anita and her father were still missing. On the third day, they were pulled from the rubble of the collapsed office building. Her father had died, and Anita was severely injured, but alive. During the public burial ceremony, loudspeakers and the radios boomed the Nazi officials' speeches. They assured everyone that the sacrifices of the three hundred bombing victims and the iron-will of each citizen spelled victory and an honorable closure to the war. Weeks had passed before we were allowed to see Anita. A nun told Emma and me, "Anita knows that she will never walk again because her spine was injured. Her broken arms are in a cast. She needs our emotional support if she is to survive. You may go in, one at a time."

I steeled myself before I entered, but I didn't expect to see a skeleton image of what once had been Anita. Her eyes had sunk into their sockets, her cheeks were hollow, her skin looked waxen, and a grayish-white arm cast kept her arms away from her sides. I didn't dare to touch her, so I caressed her cast.

"Anita, I choked, I'm so sorry." I couldn't go on.

"I know," she said. "But . . . tell me, tell me . . .why did you turn back and not come with me?"

I thought back. "I don't know. I just felt I should go back."

"I have been thinking about that. I'm glad you did leave, or you would be with Papa or here with me." She paused. "They tell me I should fight to live, but why should I want to live? Mama died a long time ago, and now, Papa is gone too. Before he died, he told me to be brave, but I am not brave. Look at me, I'm helpless. I don't want to live like that. All I want is that it is over soon."

I knew what the nun had said. Wordlessly, I placed my face against her cheek and our tears mingled. I didn't want to leave, but I didn't want to tire Anita.

"Emma is outside. She wants to see you, too."

Anita nodded weakly. I waved and left before she could hear my sobs that made me tremble.

With each visit, we could see that Anita's health failed rapidly, and her death wish became more intense. When we brought a bouquet of colorful fall flowers, she smiled weakly. "Next week is my seventeenth birthday. I want to celebrate it in heaven, with Mama and Papa."

Anita looked so frail. I knew my hugging her would cause her pain, so I patted her cast. All the while, deep anger rose within me. Why did these Americans fly in and bomb us and kill or hurt people like Anita who had just lived and worked here? When Emma, returned, she was crying.

I was still angry. "I wonder how these men feel? They must feel big when they release their bombs," I cried out. "They must know that they don't always hit the military targets, in fact, their bombs burn and kill mainly women and children. You know, when they fly away, they should have the maimed victims etched in their mind for life. Someday, they should have to care for the victims they leave behind. Tell me, Emma, will these men burn in hell some day?"

"Anneliese, this is war," Emma consoled. "Pierre said we should have seen what our soldiers and bombers did in France, in England and Russia. Pierre feels that it is the leaders of a country who decide how we live, how to make war, and when to make peace. They keep their loved ones safe, but we, the 'little people,' have no say!"

"I wish the war would end. I hate war!" I shouted.

"The only good thing that came out of this war for me," Emma said, "is the fact that I met Pierre."

"Emma, you better see the doctor soon," I said, " because I think syphilis has gone to your head."

Two days later, Anita died. I told Emma after the memorial service, "Anita was an angel. Why did she have to suffer like that? If we are bombed again and I die, tell my Mama not to cry. I don't want to suffer, nor do I want to be paralyzed like Anita had been. If that happens to me, I want to be dead."

The war intensified. Several bombings followed. Mama wrote that Cousin Hans was on the front line in Italy, and Cousin Alfred's unit was near Stalingrad when he was declared missing in action. My sympathy for Aunt Lore grew with every letter she wrote, but in her most recent one she revealed her desperate situation:

Dearest Anneliese,

The war is taking all we ever had. Your Uncle Anton and I were forced to share our home with a homeless woman and her six children. Anneliese, you would not recognize our home. The housing office furnished bunk beds, and we gave them good furnishings, which now, are scratched and nicked. The hardwood floors are always dirty, and their soiled clothing is strewn everywhere. Simply, we have no privacy. Your Uncle Anton is growing weaker and more dependent since his good lung is filling up with fluid. Yet, we could cope with all of this, if we only knew that our Alfred is going to return from Russia. There is no joy. There is no future. There is no life left if Alfred doesn't come home.

Stay well, your Aunt Lore

When Alfred was declared missing in action near Stalingrad, Aunt Lore suffered periods of deep depression, which became long-term when Uncle Anton died shortly before Christmas. Immediately after his funeral, Aunt Lore withdrew from everyone, and she made it known that she was not seeing anyone throughout the holiday season.

**My last time with Papa
Christmas 1943**

**Standing from right to left: Resi, Max and me
Sitting: Mama, Irmgard and Papa**

CHAPTER FIFTEEN

MY LAST TIME WITH PAPA

Emma offered a trade: three days of her Christmas leave, which I could repay by changing to night shifts whenever Pierre and she could be together. I thought of the risks for Emma, but for me, it meant Christmas at home with Papa and my family.

I wrote Mama that I would walk home from Wiesau. Surely, no one would hurt me — not on the night before Christmas. After I left the Wiesau station shortly after midnight, I pushed on and took the shortcut through the woods. I was tired and tense, but I watched and listened as with each step the hard crust of snow crackled under my feet. Suddenly, in the distance I saw a dark spot moving toward me — my heart pounded wildly — it was a man. I left the path determined to outrun him.

The man called out, "Don't you run away from me! Come on, now don't you run away from me!"

Gathering all my strength I dashed . . . I dashed right into his open arms. I pounded his chest and shouted, "Papa, Papa where did you come from?"

"From home. Do you think your Mama would let me sleep while you are roaming through the woods at midnight?"

"You scared me!"

"Can't say that I am sorry. Tell me, what must we do so you won't walk in these woods alone?"

"Papa, I wanted to be home when you got there."

We walked quietly side by side. It was so good to have Papa here with me. Momentarily, I forgot about the war, my work, and the cramped quarters at home.

Papa broke the silence. "Anneliese, we will want to make our time together count, so let us talk now and forget our worries over the holidays. Your Mama never complains. Uncle Anton's death, having renters, and worrying about us must be taking its toll."

"Now that food rations have become more irregular, Mama wants the toolshed made into a small barn for a goat and two kids, a few chickens, and two rabbits. Pepp has already arranged for it. He also suggested that instead of paying rent for our fields he will trade potatoes and straw. Mama feels additional milk is needed since two liters are not sufficient for a family of five. The chickens would supply eggs, and the rabbit meat would be a feast. Mama knows the risk. If someone turns her in to the authorities, she will get less rations. Pepp knows several families who have supplemented their rations for quite some time, and they feel the risk is minimal since the inspector can be bribed with food. Mama has an arrangement with Mrs. Dimpfl which will keep starvation from everyone's door. Mrs. Dimpfl will help Mama with the work if she can feed a rabbit or two and get some goat milk for her children."

"Papa, nothing is the same anymore, is it?"

"No, you are seventeen, so you need to understand that, sometimes, you must do things you never thought of doing just to survive. It is all right as long as you don't hurt anyone else in the process. What your mama is doing takes planning, and fortitude. We are lucky because, without her, our life would not be of the same quality. You, Resi, Max, Irmgard, and most of all, I, owe her for our well-being. Don't you ever forget, she has always put her family first."

"Papa, I know, but I have nothing to give her for Christmas. Nothing." I cried out.

"We have each other, and we are still in our own home, so don't be childish and fret about gifts," Papa scolded lightly.

Despite the lack of special gifts, we held onto the warmth and special glow of Christmas 1943. We stayed near Mama and Papa as Grandma led her extended family to the Midnight mass. Uncle Pepp, Papa and Uncle Franz lit a Christmas candle and prayed for our soldiers' safety. I watched Mrs. Beer and Maria as they stood by the Patron Saint of Travelers Statue, Saint Christopher, with their heads bowed, deep in prayer. They repeatedly turned to the East, West, and South, the directions in which her sons served. After church, Mama and I waited and we joined the two women at the exit.

Mrs. Beer, though tears glistened in her eyes, nodded toward me. She greeted Mama and said, "Peppi, Max spoke to me earlier, and he told me that you have your family home."

Mama took Mrs. Beer's hand and they stepped aside. I faced Maria. For loss of words, I stammered, "Maria, a blessed Christmas."

"Mama wouldn't agree," she sighed, "but I say it isn't. You know Josef died; Otto is in a Russian prison camp, critically wounded. Max and Martin were critically wounded also, and they are in field hospitals near the front. Franz, so far, is the lucky one — he is in France."

I hugged her. "Maria, I said a prayer for you. How can I help?"

"If only I could go with you and escape the hell around our house. Herman will be sixteen next month, and he talks of nothing but enlisting. Of course, Herman knows that this kind of talk infuriates Papa. Mama cries, the little ones are upset, and the foreign workers talk to each other, all at once. Sometimes I think of running away, because I can't stand it much longer. Then I think of Mama and wonder, 'Why is God punishing Mama so?' All she does is work and worry about her men." Maria covered her eyes and stroked her forehead. "I should get going and get the girls to bed before Mama gets home. Write to me, will you?" We took leave and I walked away. Resi, Irmgard and Max passed me, gliding, falling and laughing, they relished being out on Christmas Eve.

Papa said, "Let's walk slowly, so Mama can catch up." He turned toward me. "I take it Maria told you about her brothers?"

"Yes, she did."

Papa took my hand. "How blessed we are," he said with finality.

As I entered the kitchen early Christmas morning, Papa sat by the radio. He laid his finger on his lips and kept his ear pressed firmly against the cloth-covered speaker. Mama stood by the stove, and I sat still while he listened intently to the barely audible voice of the announcer.

"Kiev . . . Italy . . . encircled tanks . . ." Who is speaking? I wondered.

After a while Papa turned the radio off.

"Max," Mama said, "I wish you would forget about these stations." She pointed at little Max asleep on the sofa. "He is such a little boy. If he mentioned anywhere that you are listening to London or any other foreign station, you know the consequences. A fine time we would have trying to visit you in prison."

"Peppi," Papa cajoled. "Look at him. He sleeps the sleep of the dead. I had it so low and I bet, even you couldn't tell me what was said."

"I don't want to know. Whatever he says is probably as much propaganda as we hear. If not, just what can you do about the war here? Especially, if they take you away to prison? I wish you would forget about these broadcasts."

"Peppi, you have to hear both sides and then make up your own mind. Anyway, London is more truthful than what we hear. Our stations?" Papa shook his head. "They feed us half-truths, the propaganda they feed us."

I didn't like what Papa was doing. Since he listened every morning, Mama and I had more things to worry about. What if they arrested Papa? How were we going to survive the shame? I wondered.

The holidays were over, and it was time for me to say good-bye. At Uncle Pepp's, Aunt Nannie, Erna, and all the workers sat around the big table, talking and watching while Kasha, Babette, and Maria offered steaming hot dumplings. I stood aside when the door opened wide; Sepp, Michael and Herbert decked out in their SA uniforms stood there. Sepp stepped forward, slammed his boots together and the threesome chorused, "Heil Hitler!"

All activity ceased, all eyes were fixed on Uncle Pepp as he asked, "What brings you here?"

"Pepp," Sepp said curtly. "Now I have seen it with my own eyes. The foreign laborers sit with you and your family at **your** table. Don't you know they are **not** your equals?"

"It says right here." He held a pamphlet up and read, "'Be courteous, but a foreigner **can not** be treated like a German.'"

"Pepp, I hear you treat them as well, or even better than German workers have it elsewhere. Foreign laborers must not break bread with you. That practice must stop, or I will take all your foreign workers back to camp."

Uncle Pepp had listened quietly. He rose. "Are you through?" His voice was like ice. "Sepp, you never had much of a brain in school, and it seems your brain has shrunk since you left there. **Listen**! These workers work for me!" His fist hit the table. "**They work harder than you ever could stand!** I must bake bread for the town and half the county and you come in here and tell me you must take these workers back to camp? Well, go ahead, why don't you? I, in turn, will close my bakery. You take my workers . . . I can't bake."

Uncle Pepp moved toward Sepp, until they were nose to nose, "Just remember, I tried to tell you. When there is no bread tomorrow and the next day, and the next, you will have some explaining to do to our mayor and the people of this town. Maybe you and your comrades here can take my workers' places and bake. Now, don't waste my time. Take the workers with you, or get out of my way. Unlike you, we have work to do as soon as we eat our cold food."

I had never seen Uncle Pepp so tall, and it seemed Sepp and his comrades hadn't either. They looked at Sepp and conferred.

"Pepp, you know I must follow my superior's orders without doing special favors for anyone," Sepp whined. "We are at war with those people, we can't let everything go by, and . . ."

Uncle Pepp interrupted. "As I said, we have to get back to work."

His face beet red, Sepp and his subdued comrades turned and left without another word.

Wiedold, who understood German, said, "Thank you. We won't forget."

Uncle Pepp gave a slight wave with his hand, as if he wanted to erase the whole episode. Everyone was talking at once. I said good-bye to an Uncle Pepp I had not seen before, and I wondered if he would hear from Sepp again.

Papa expertly took charge and started work transforming his tool shed into a barn. Turning toward me he said, "The next time you come home, your mama will be a farmer."

"When you're ready," Papa said, "I'll walk with you." I looked forward to our walk to Wiesau because it prolonged my time with Papa before I returned to Regensburg and he to Berlin where war broke through the sky at will. He listened quietly while I told him about my work, the Lehnerts and how deeply I felt the cruel death of

Anita.

"Papa," I asked, "Why do some people suffer so? Look at
Maria's mama, Aunt Lore, . . . Anita, or all the little children and
apprentices who died. It just is not fair."

"As long as I can remember, Anneliese, you always wanted
everything fair. Haven't you learned anything during this time of
war? Especially during war time, people all over the world live with
unfairness. Don't you remember? It was a long time ago . . . you were
about eight when, within a month, four of your classmates died of
diphtheria, and another one died because she had diabetes. You were
scared that you would die too, and at the same time you were very
angry because it was so unfair. It was then that I told you that people
were like pebbles in the sand. Do you remember?"

"Yes, but tell me again," I pleaded.

"You always liked my stories, but did you learn anything?
Listen."

"You are in a world of pebbles where some beautiful
pebbles lie near or under rough, dull pebbles in the
sand. It is because of where they are that they'll never
have a chance to come to the top. Someone steps on
them and keeps them down until they lie still. Yet,
there are other pebbles. They are on the surface and
the sun shines upon them until they glisten. Someone
may pick them up, polish them and shape them until
they are as bright and beautiful as they can be. Some
of these pebbles get selfish, and they never do
anything but glisten. But there are others who bring
joy to children and everyone around them.

Some pebbles can be bought for a great deal of
money. Their owners may use them for good causes,
or they may use them for their own pleasures until they
lose their shine or value. Then they take these pebbles
and throw them back into the sea, or push them into the
surface sand so deeply that no one can retrieve them.
Anneliese, the world is filled with pebbles yet, there
are not two pebbles alike. Each one has a different
shape, some are of a different color, but each pebble

has its own story and its own place on the beach of life. Many could tell you their stories, and then you would know what happened was not fair, but nevertheless, they all had a purpose for being."

As always, Papa made things more acceptable. When I asked him what kind of pebble he thought I was, he smiled and said, "I might have answered that question when you were eight, but now, you just have to think about that and work on the kind of pebble you want to be. You know, I had so many plans, and I envisioned what the future would hold for you, matter of fact, for all of us. But there again, I learned from the old folk saying. 'Man thinks and plans, but God does the stirring.'"

"But then, Papa, why should I try to do anything?"

"You know the answer," Papa reprimanded. "You are put on this earth, to use what God gave you, and to do the best you can."

Soon we saw the outskirts of Wiesau. "Anneliese, you are leaving for Regensburg and within a few days I will be back in Berlin. Since the air raids become more frequent with each passing day, we don't know when we will see each other again. You are seventeen. Times are hard and so uncertain, but we taught you to do right, so don't willfully cause hurt for anyone. If you do, you will pay sooner or later. Your grandmother always told Pepp and me these truths: 'If you willfully dig a grave for someone, you will fall in yourself.' You don't have to get even with anyone who hurt you because, 'God's mills grind slowly, but surely, and 'if you tell one lie, you'll always have to tell another lie to cover the first one. Soon, the lie owns you, but the truth frees you.' Believe me. It is so. Live by these old truths, and you will do well."

Suddenly, he stopped. He reached for me, and hugged me. "I am going back," he said. "God willing, we will see each other again." He held me tight for a moment longer. Then he took my face between his hands. He kissed me on the cheek, and in sorrow held my gaze until, gently, he pushed me away und urged, "Go, go on my dear. May your Guardian Angels keep you under their wings and may God be with you, and keep you safe," he whispered as he abruptly turned and left.

I stood there, and I cried out, "Papa, Papa, please don't leave me yet!"

Papa looked at me, "Anneliese," he said, "I will never leave you."

"But Papa—"

"Anneliese" he broke in, "you will remember what I said, and you will do things like I taught you. So you see, I will be with you more often than you know."

He kicked a solitary tree trunk and stomped straight ahead. He didn't look back until he came to the woods and then it was too late for him to see my tears. The tall, ancient fir trees shrouded him and I could see him no more.

CHAPTER SIXTEEN

VICTORY LOST

During winter and spring our soldiers were losing their grip on the Russian land and its people. Ever since the loss of Stalingrad during February of 1943, the enemy tenaciously inched west. Deep within, we realized that our soldiers, these ghost-like shapes, draped in white rags, were not regrouping — they were retreating from the enemy who drove them toward our borders. Although the frigid blanket of ice and snow was absent in Italy and France, there, too, our soldiers were beaten into retreat.

At home the war took its toll on families. Maria's brother, Herman, barely sixteen, had joined the Army. The Beer family had lost two sons and they prayed and worried over four soldier sons on battlefields East and West. Numerous wives and mothers were now heads of households because their husbands or sons had died on the fronts.

Mama wrote that the bakery manager, Cousin Karl, and Uncle Pepp fought their own war: Karl had not worried after he received his draft notice because Pepp needed him; surely, he would petition his draft. But Uncle Pepp didn't.

"Karl got along fine when he joined the Nazi Party in 1936," Uncle Pepp said. "Everyone in the family told me then, 'Pepp, let him be, Karl is his own man, and he can make his own decisions. I am not stepping in now. Karl was his own man then, and I say he is his own man now."

No one could change Uncle Pepp's mind. Whenever anyone approached him, he replied, "There is nothing to discuss, Karl can take care of himself."

Within two weeks Karl had been drafted and he was placed in

training with an occupational unit on its way to France.

Ilse, Karl's wife, spoke her mind to anyone listening. "Sending Karl out like that makes Pepp the likeness of Cain, and purgatory is too good for him. I hope he rots in Hell. I already worry about our two oldest. Johann is missing in Italy, and Ida is in the Women's Army Corps in Poland. With the Russians advancing every day, I can't sleep. So what does Pepp do? In his stubbornness and pride, he adds Karl to my worries. I will never forgive him for that! Never!"

Marerl was affected by the war too. She wrote:

> Can you believe it, Anneliese, I am finally free! Karola and I were drafted into the Women's Work Corps for eighteen months of compulsory service. Of course, Mrs. Luckner asked the mayor to intervene the inscription, but when he asked me, 'Marerl, you want to stay where you are, or do you want to serve your country?' I told the mayor that there was nothing more important than to serve my country. He patted me on the shoulder and said, 'What a wonderful German girl you are.' I was in! We were barely home, when Mrs. Luckner gave me the worst beating ever, but it was also the last beating I had to endure. It is a month now since I am on my own. Since we are on farms, we have more food than what the rations allow, but our sleeping quarters are without heat and we awake half frozen. While some girls complain and are homesick, for me this is heaven. No more beatings! After six months we will be transferred to Munich to work in an ammunition plant. Air raids or famine, I will go anywhere as long as I am away from her.
>
> Take care. Love, always, your friend, Marerl

We, too, were facing restrictions. Since June, everyone's leave had been canceled and we frequently worked 12-hour shifts. The Americans landed in France, and fierce fighting ensued over established beachheads, as the Americans inched their way through France on to our boarders. We listened to the news, and prayed for our loved ones.

Our director, Mrs. Hecht, made light of the somber mood that held us captive. "You blondes won't have to worry. I heard the American men love blondes, so when they come, just marry one of them and you will be safe, and you will also have a good life because nothing is destroyed in America."

"Marry an American? That will never happen!" I cried out. "They shoot at us, then they bomb us, and then we should marry them? I say, 'Never!'"

"Stranger things have happened," Mrs. Hecht reasoned.

When the long-awaited miracle weapon, V-1, did not break England's fighting spirit, our supervisor assessed his options. "I realize that presently hunger, exhaustion, and even fear of the unknown control our lives; nevertheless, I am ordered to intensify our war efforts. I could demand daily reports of your whereabouts during your free hours, but I will wait until you give me reasons to do so."

Mama wrote that Papa was still in Berlin where he had been tested for the Front Patrol Corps. This unit captured the soldiers who had left the front without leave and delivered them to a military tribunal for sentencing. Papa had failed the Front Patrol Corps test and his conscription into the Army was imminent. I couldn't understand it. Papa had never failed a test: Why would he fail one now?

CHAPTER SEVENTEEN

HELL ON EARTH — OCTOBER 1944

I was anxious — and against all existing rules, everything was arranged. I would travel to Munich and spend two days with my childhood friend, Bertl and her family. Right after I had boarded the train to Munich, I succumbed to much needed sleep. Now, awake and refreshed, I wondered what Bertl had planned.

"We will meet at the depot, Anneliese. I have the night shift, so we should be home by forenoon. Just wait until tomorrow! If we have a day without an air raid, Munich, here we come!" she exclaimed.

"Next station, Munich," the train conductor announced, and after he had everyone's attention he went on. "Ten minutes to the main railway station, everyone. No one will be allowed to remain on the train. When the train stops, leave immediately."

"Do you really think any one would want to stay in this sooty train?" a woman asked.

The conductor's reply was drowned out by the wail of a siren. *Whoowee — Whoowee.* "Air raid! Air raid!" someone shouted. I held on tightly to my small overnight case and shivered with fear. The train screeched to a stop and the abrupt silence within was suffocating. Everyone was edgy, watching, and listening.

"We are near an underground shelter," the conductor directed. "Leave the train and follow me! Hurry!"

Since I was near the exit, I felt relieved. Confidently, I moved toward the door until the passengers behind me surged forward with unbearable force.

"Please everyone, be orderly! We will make it to the shelter!" someone called out.

The sudden surge of the frantic passengers behind pushed me down the steps and onto the pavement. Terror-stricken, we ran helter-skelter along the platform to the dimly lit underground hallway. It seemed an eternity passed before a thick, luminous arrow lead us to the open shelter. This was the place where we would wait out the air raid. The pushing, elbowing and shoving continued until we who were in front were swallowed up in the cavity of the huge underground cavern. People poured in from all sides, and in a moment, the area was filled with sweaty people hot with fear.

The conductor called out, "No more! Stand back now. Stand back!" The unlucky masses who could not get in protested their fate because they were destined to stay in the tunnel's passageway. I stared in fright as the ponderous, wooden door clanked shut with a thud and two men braced it cross-wise with steel bars. A damp haze hung over the huge shelter and several huge flashlights cast a bleak pallor on the walls. Whenever someone moved, their grotesque shadow gave the shelter an unearthly atmosphere.

Near me, several elderly ladies turned their eyes upward. "Please, Father, have our Guardian Angels keep us under their wings. Bless us and forgive us our sins," they prayed and they sought comfort in their rosaries, marking each bead while it slid through their gnarled fingers.

On the other side of the tunnel, a child cried, "Mama, I want to go home! I want to go home, now!"

"Sh, sh," its mother urged in a soothing voice.

Some people talked in low voices while others stood and stared or sat and cried. We waited. Suddenly, panic and fear gripped me like a vice. I had been in air raids in Regensburg; the people in the telegraph office shelters were my friends, but here, surrounded by strangers, I felt a sickening aloneness. I hadn't told anyone that I planned to visit Bertl. If I died, not even Bertl would know what happened to me, and I would be left to rot in the rubble and cease to exist.

I huddled down by a stone pillar remembering Papa's advice, "Anneliese, during an air raid, always sit near the reinforcement of a door or the ceiling."

The planes arrived and droned on and on. "Get ready for a big one," someone said.

The endless moan of the planes' approach, a never-ending *OOOOOHH*, confirmed everyone's worst fear --- an exceptionally heavy bomb run was in store for us. The sound of a nose dive was immediately followed by the ear-shattering *KA-WHOOMP* of bombs smashing everything in their wake. These sounds were repeated without a pause, again and again as the planes zoomed in low and unloaded their deadly cargo.

The anti-aircraft guns barked. Bombs exploded and the bombers returned to the sky.

The rain of bombs, the deafening sounds whistled and boomed down from above and filled the tunnel with their relentless madness: lights flickered; wide-eyed children shook in terror, whimpered and cried as their mothers anguished at being powerless to stop the terror. They covered their babies with their bodies.

"Everyone, be still and conserve oxygen for our survival," the conductor blared over a loudspeaker. "We must preserve oxygen!"

All madness broke loose as wave after wave of planes continuously sought their targets. Each time a plane dropped its explosive mines and fire bombs, the stone walls of the tunnel shuddered as if they were made of flimsy paper and the ground below heaved in protest to the assault.

I pushed myself against the stone pillar and covered my ears. The steel braces on the door buckled some with every explosion, and the flashlights clattered to the floor until we were in semi-darkness.

"Oh, God, don't bury us here! Please!" I cried. The terror of being buried alive crept into my consciousness, uncontrollable fear overtook me, and I was screaming.

A woman next to me moved closer. She put her arms around my shoulder and said, "Just hold on."

I buried my head in her lap and closed my eyes tightly. My teeth chattered ... my whole body shook uncontrollably as the loud droning abated and finally faded into nothingness. The bombs had found their mark and danger had passed.

Suddenly an uncanny stillness settled over everything. The abrupt silence was as disturbing as the sounds of the bombers. Now the wondering and the waiting began. Had we survived the raid, or was that just a momentary reprieve before yet another onslaught would start?

Time passed slowly. Some people talked quietly while others sat inert, bomb-sodden. We waited for ten minutes ... half an hour, but the "All Clear" signal did not come.

A soldier across from us cursed out, "Damn it! I'd sooner be at the front, out in the open. On the front we fight man to man, and we can see what is coming at us, but here, the front line is made up of women and children, herded underground, to die like moles." He held his head and covered his face with his hands and sobbed.

The women next to me tried to distract me from my fear. "You aren't from here, are you?"

"No, I just came to visit a friend."

"You will," she reassured me, "even if they come again. This is a good shelter. I always come here." She looked up and listened. "Here they come again. Today they carpet bomb. They'll continue where they left off, so we'll be in for it."

This time the flak guns were still, and the planes came in unopposed. Wave upon wave of planes came in low and released explosive and fire bombs directly above us. The noise; screaming, crying, praying, and the sound of bombs exploding, was deafening and the pain in my head was unbearable. I felt my heart would explode through my ears any minute now.

I screamed from the pain in my head, I cowered near the ground and covered my head with my hands.

"Please, stop!" I cried out, "stop the pain!"

Finally, stillness came. The woman next to me moved her lips, but in a stupor, I could not understand what she said. We sat sullen, zombie-like, staring blankly. We waited as we recuperated, but we were afraid to move for fear that the Allies were not through with us yet.

"My ears ache so and I can barely hear anything," I said. "You have hearing loss, but the pain will get better. Just sit still," the woman near me said. She turned toward me and pinched my nostrils. "Now breathe in and hold your breath. There, did your ear drum crack? Let's do it again." After several more tries, she inquired, "Can you hear me now?"

"Yes! Barely, but I can hear." I pressed her hand gratefully.

"We'll be able to leave shortly. Let's hope they're done for today. It will not be a pretty sight up there."

We leaned against each other and rested uneasily until the "All Clear" signal sounded and the door opened. People moved; strangers hugged each other, others chattered, cried without restraint, or giggled shrilly. We had made it through the noon hours while upstairs a monster had devoured civilization. We could breath, and we could leave the tunnel.

I clutched my small suitcase. This time no one pushed because we were not eager to walk into chaos. Someone said, "Now we will see hell out there, hell on earth!"

As we reached the top of the stairs, we could not see the once cloudless sky. Huge, orange napalm-fires and black billows of smoke rose above the skyline, their sharp, pungent smell gagged me, my nostrils clogged until I coughed uncontrollably.

"Oh, this is bad," the woman said. She broke into a run and she disappeared among the rubble and smoke.

"Wait, what is your name? " I yelled into the chaos. "I want to thank you! Where can I go now?"

The railroad tracks where we had disembarked hours ago were a grotesquerie of steel rearing up against the madness of the murky, orange fire monster that rose and fell in the sky. I tried not to look at the gaunt railroad-car skeletons that smoldered and burned. I shivered, and yet I was sweating because the high wind and the heat were unbearable. Workers, their faces blackened by soot, dashed here and there and worked feverishly as they roped off areas where the less-fortunate passengers had been caught in the inferno of the bombing raid. The sickly-sweet smell of burnt flesh and death hung over the workers. Some unlucky enough to survive the flames screamed in pain as phosphorous liquid burnt their skin, melted their flesh, and exposed their bones. Others agonized and cried for death. Workers hurried to help as best they could, but the dead — the dead were the most horrible sight. I stood in a stupor while a group of old men piled the dead like cordwood.

"Just keep the ones with their metal identification tag," the depot warden instructed, "and take the corpses without a tag and pile them up here until the wagon comes."

Groping my way around craters, mountains of rubble and ruins of burnt out homes, I followed the paths that strangers near me had made. Survivors crawled out of bombed-out caverns, staring

Surviving residents returned from bomb shelters to the above.

blankly into the distance, clutching their belongings in their hands. Some were lifted out of the rubble and sat in shock, while others salvaged what they could in a frenzy. The dense smoke and the foul air still had me gasping for breath. The involuntary coughing spells persisted and racked my body, bile stuck in my throat, and a wave of nausea lasted until I was drained and weak. From my retching, my head pounded and pounded. I couldn't stand this havoc any longer, I had to get back to Regensburg. Surging forward, I trembled in fear of the unrelenting power of the enemy I had not seen and did not know.

I rushed up to a passerby who carried clothing in a basket. "I must get back to Regensburg. Please, how can I get away?"

"You may have to go several miles before you get out of the bombed-out area. You must follow the trolley tracks where you can find them and make connections from there," he said as he hurried on.

"Thank you," I hollered as his silhouette rushed through the destruction.

I walked for blocks without finding the tracks. "I must find them. I must find them," I muttered aloud to myself.

In the bombed-out areas, survivors rummaged through the rubble and the skeletons of buildings. An elderly woman sat on a pile of bricks and cried out to her neighbor, "I have nothing left! All is gone! My poor Fritz is on the front and my poor children . . . are dead. Now I want to die."

I stopped near a woman and called out, "Where can I find a trolley? I must get back to Regensburg."

The woman kept digging and without looking up at me said, "Just go ahead for a few more blocks. It should get better. Someone said the trolleys run there. Just see that you get out of here before the planes come back again."

"Please, God! No!" I gasped and I started to run and stumble over the debris.

Fear pushed me until I felt exhausted and faint. I had not eaten, nor had I slept since last night. Finally, the paths were streets again and I heard the rumble of the trolley cars in the distance. It wasn't long before the trolley came into view.

"Here it is! I found it," I wept while I ran for the trolley.

People moved forward as the trolley came to a stop. I pushed and shoved with everyone until I reached the top platform. Within minutes, we rode past unfamiliar houses and streets until we reached the depot of Munich-Gemering. Several passengers pointed to the makeshift information booth where crude, black letters stated, "Departure for Regensburg at 3:00 p.m. Track will be announced."

"Stay near the tracks, outside. That way you will get on the train," someone said.

I gingerly stepped over and around the tired travelers who sat on benches or reclined as best they could on the tiled platform. I searched for a space on a bench, but all that was left was the tile. Resolutely, I sat down, I propping my small night case against my back and resting my eyes, until the anxious wakefulness of the past hours took its toll. I was dozing fitfully when the conductor's booming voice woke me.

"Train departure to Regensburg and north will be imminent if we can locate an engine." Speaking to no one in particular, he added, "Turn right; follow the signs for Track Eight."

Fatigued bodies moved lethargically, gathered their ragged baggage, and followed a nameless leader. Luck was with us as we boarded a vacant coach. Most passengers wrestled forward and hustled for an aisle seat. An aisle seat gave more protection during air attacks and the path to the exits was immediately accessible. I could push no more, so I settled down by a window. My thoughts turned to Bertl and I wondered how she had fared. If her workplace had withstood the bombing, she could not leave until the next shift arrived. Somehow, I had to get in touch with her.

The coach jerked and lurched forward. "Well, look at that!" someone exclaimed. "They found an engine!"

After a few false starts, the train slowly picked up speed and the view of Munich soon faded in the distance. Some passengers slept. Others sat apathetically and kept their thoughts to themselves. A group of soldiers on their way back to the front fervently voiced their concerns. The news reports for the front-line soldiers always emphasized that their patriotism and bravery protected their families. They could only suspect what was taking place within the boundaries of the Fatherland because letters to the front were censored. Last night, they had lived through and felt the destructive power of the American Air Force and had learned that their loved ones lived with the constant horrors of bombing, fire, and death.

"We must have faith in our Fuhrer," an officer interjected. "We will get our new wonder weapon going again and then, we will annihilate the British. They will pay and pay!"

"I hope that will happen soon, sir. How much more can our families take?" a soldier quietly commented.

It was evening when our train arrived in Regensburg. As I walked slowly through streets untouched by horror bombings, my apprehension diminished and sudden tiredness overtook me. Hoping for a night of uninterrupted sleep, I entered my room. Relishing the rays of the setting sun and the cool breeze which came through the windows, I sat quietly, resting.

The shrill ring of the phone brought me up with a start. Bertl was on the other end. "Anneliese, we worried about you. I am so glad you are home. Where were you during the raid? The depot was an inferno!"

"Yes, Bertl, I was in a shelter at the depot, and it was horrendous. I was so terrified that I could not stay in Munich one minute longer. How do you take it, Bertl?"

"Anneliese, the Munich we knew is gone — it is a town of death!" Bertl lowered her voice, "Our manager said that at least three hundred residents died last night, over 10,000 are homeless, and we are without water and gas. You and I were the lucky ones — we survived. The hotel was not damaged except for some broken windows. We will replace them with cardboard. They tell me the trolleys are out, so that means I will have to stay at work. Don't worry about me, we are safe in the telegraph building. We have only one emergency line working, so bye, and don't let the Yankees get you."

Just then Emma, my co-worker, burst in. "Get off the phone, Anneliese, I just heard the dairy received a shipment of eggs and they will be sold early, tomorrow morning. Let's beat the line. Since I am scheduled to work through the night, will you meet me at seven? By the way, I came over earlier, but you were out."

I trembled, as I remembered the terror of the night, and I could not speak of it. "I will be ready in the morning," I promised. "Hopefully, we will get there before they run out."

Survivors of "carpet bombings" have orientation problems as they search for their homes.

CHAPTER EIGHTEEN

TOMORROW MAY NEVER COME

The early morning sky was bleak. We were three blocks from the store, and, already, a line three-abreast was strung out ahead of us. "It has been two months since we had eggs," Emma said. "I just hope they won't run out before we get into the store."

The line moved at a snail's pace and everyone was anxious and on edge. Whenever a group of people left the store, we listened and watched them intently as they carefully carried their treasure: two eggs for each card holder.

"How many crates of eggs are left in the store?" someone asked.

"Mr. Kohl told me," a woman responded, "that for once he has enough. The trucker couldn't get the eggs to Stuttgart because Munich and towns in the surrounding counties were bombed last night, so you are in luck. All you have to do is wait."

The assurance of enough eggs lifted everyone's spirits. If the sirens did not disband us to the bomb shelters, time and discomfort did not matter now. In the past, just when we thought the waiting in line was over, the stores ran out of food. That meant anxiety and more waiting until food was available again, but today, we were in luck. The clerk took my stamps, checked them carefully, and handed me two eggs. Now, all I wanted was to get home safely with my precious food.

"Anneliese, let's go to your place and eat our eggs as soon as we get there," Emma suggested.

"No, Emma, I am not going to do that. Mama gave me more than enough egg-keeper solution so I am going to preserve my eggs. If you want, we can share the egg-keeper."

"That's not necessary. I know eating an omelet is sinful, but my eggs will not see tomorrow. Why wait until the Yankees get your eggs?" Emma turned to go. "How I wish I had your will power!"

After I completed some long-overdue errands, it was evening, and I was alone. Because of the bombings, total blackout was the law. I pulled the window shades and fastened them to the window frames so the lights wouldn't shine through. My small bed lamp gave the room a soothing glow while I relished each bite of a slice of sourdough bread and fifty grams of cottage cheese. Dried apple peelings steeping in a cup of water gave me a semblance of tea. My mind was frequently on my eggs, which I had squirreled away in the wardrobe across the room. I went and checked. Yes, the eggs were in the egg-keeper, and the small crock was securely stored under the bottom shelf.

My landlord, Mr. Lehnert, came to the door. "Anneliese, would you like today's newspaper?" he inquired. "You were not here yesterday so you missed hours in the shelter. Good for you. We heard that the bombers targeted Munich."

"I didn't miss it. I was in Munich."

"That must have been horrendous."

"It was," I said.

"Well, the paper said the Americans did a lot of damage during the two hour raid. I guess their main target was the depot in the center of the city. You are all right?"

"Yes, I hope they let us sleep tonight."

"Well, read the paper and go to sleep. Hanna and I worried about you."

"Thanks for the paper," I called out as he closed the door.

I moved my small lamp to the headboard of the bed, propped up the pillows, and crawled in.

I scanned the headlines, but only the back page of the paper gave scant information.

TERROR AIR RAID OVER MUNICH AND
SURROUNDING COUNTIES.
294 planes Type Lancaster and numerous Type
B17-S selected Munich for their target. Due to the
excellent and courageous defense of our flak units the

backup wave of bombers failed. They did not reach·
their targets as planned and the planes dropped their
bombs at random over small towns and villages in the
area, and again, the war mongers added another act of
inhumanity.

"Did that reporter miss the second onslaught of the bomb
run?" I wondered aloud as flashes of broken bodies and the whistling
sounds of bombs robbed me of sleep. I tossed and turned and I
thought, "What if they bomb tonight? My eggs will crack, burst, or
worse yet, break! Why save them? Why not eat them right now!"

I left my bed, retrieved my eggs and cupped them in my
hands. I sat down by the closet and scolded myself. "Don't go crazy,
Anneliese. Put the eggs back! You had bread and cheese tonight.
Stay within your rations; save the eggs. You might get sick. Then it
will be good to have them."

I walked back and forth in my room and reasoned, "The eggs
will be closer to me on the night stand where I can just grab them and
run to the shelter with the first wail of the siren. Then they will be
safe."

Now that my eggs were safe on the night stand, I crawled into
bed, and concentrated on sleep. It was no use. My mind raced.
"What if they bomb? I could just eat one egg and save the other for
an emergency. That is what I will do."

I ran across the cold wooden floor, and lit the small gas burner
on the table. I watched with glee as the blue flame sprang to life. My
mouth watered in anticipation while the water in the frying pan
bubbled to a boil and the small, blue flame danced below.

"I will scramble the egg into water and so I will have more,"
I whispered.

The eggshell cracked easily on the side of the pan and the
bubbles of the water reached out and almost congealed the egg white.
I burst the yolk and stirred until the water, whites, and yolk were one.
The aroma of the egg penetrated my nostrils and I happily teased my
taste buds with the first bite. It tasted even better than I remembered.
My will power dissipated; crack, glide — Egg Number Two was now
in the frying pan. I smashed the yolk, stirred rapidly, slurped the soft
egg, and scraped the fry pan until it was shiny clean.

The empty space where the eggs had been glared at me. I felt disheartened and angry with myself and I blurted out, "So much for your will power, Anneliese! You couldn't keep your eggs, not even for one night! What will you do now? What if you get sick? What will you do then?"

I left the table, shuffled to my bed, and turned out the light. I slid under the down cover until I was surrounded by darkness. I punched my pillows and wept until I fell into a fitful sleep.

CHAPTER NINETEEN

1945 — GOING HOME

As the Allied troops of the East and West continued their advance toward our borders, Adolf Hitler proclaimed the "People's Defense of the German Land." Immediately, boys, sixteen, and men in their sixties were inducted into the "People's Army" and, without sufficient training, they were declared combat ready.

Despite the total home mobilization, the sky over Germany was punctured at will by American and British planes bombing Berlin, or Hamburg, Coblenz, or Munich. Slowly, all around us, the unmistakable truth became evident: as long as Germany refused to surrender, death and indescribable hardships were part of our daily struggle for survival. Our Munich telegraph connection was off frequently, and during December, telegraphers became bold and keyed over the wires, "Munich joins Hamburg, Nuremberg, and many other cities which have ceased to exist, and everyday, we live with death and destruction, . . . we hope that the end of the war will come soon, anything is better than this! To keep some normalcy until that day comes, we'll do what we can at work, if the American and British bombers don't kill us first."

It was Christmas, but when we looked around us, everything belied its meaning. Bavaria, the heart of Germany, had become the safety Mecca for throngs of refugees who had fled before the Russians took their villages and towns. Many told stories of rape, forced slave labor, cruelty, and utter despair.

Here and there mothers, some stoic, others desperately crying out, came to newly created orphanages and searched for children they had lost while fleeing the front. I thought of Kasha, Wiedold, Maria, Roman, and yes, Pierre, and wondered what their trek into Germany had been like.

Within all this chaos I heard from Marerl and I was more concerned for her safety than ever.

Our barracks had been severely damaged during several air raids and all of Munich was in disarray, she wrote. We were homeless for days, so several of my comrades and I left Munich and walked toward home. But, days later, the military police picked us up, and we were arrested for being AWOL. Immediately, we were subjected to a public court hearing and after hours of interrogation we were dishonored as traitors. Believe me, Anneliese, I was scared. Crowds watched. Some cheered, others were silent while our emblems were torn from our uniforms, and we were sentenced to six months heavy labor in a U-boat mine factory.

Suddenly our damaged barracks looked like castles. Hunger was constant. The SS Guards kept most food rations and embezzled our substandard pay. We were treated worse than the foreign laborers, since they wanted to make an example of us. Finally, my time was up, and I was returned to my former unit. I hope you will receive this letter, so someone knows I'm still alive. I'll tell you though, I have learned a great deal about survival, and if Munich is bombed and we are without shelter, I will run away again.

Stay well and safe, always, your friend, Marerl

I wondered aloud, "Marerl, when will your life change for the better?"

It was a warm mid-February day when Emma and I were walking to work. The shrillness of the air raid siren broke our pace and we followed several strangers as we ran for the nearest bomb shelter. Before we could reach it, fighter planes zoomed down from the cloudless sky and bullets whizzed by. Instinctively, I felt my cheek and brushed my hand across my arm. I was all right. We ran, and I felt as though my lungs could burst when suddenly, once more, the fighter planes zoomed down, released their bullets and disappeared beyond the blue sky.

I grabbed Emma and we reached the locked shelter entrance as the bombers released their deadly load. Shaking with fright I leaned against the wall, slid down and crouched on the floor. Screaming engines and loud explosions shook the earth repeatedly until finally it subsided. My ears hurt like they had during the Munich raid, and deafness shut out the sounds while we trembled with each shock. Finally, the raid was over.

I pointed west. Smoke rose from the Messerschmitt plant, and the bridge we had passed was a pile of rubble. I felt deep anger. "Emma," I said, "there they were, high up in the sky and they swooped down and shot at us? What have we done to them?"

Emma shrugged, "Pierre says that is war, we don't have to do anything. It's just where you are when a war starts."

The bridge was closed and we were directed to a detour, but not before we had seen the men in striped prison uniforms. They were skeleton-like figures, with their heads shaven. No one spoke, they worked, their heads bent, while armed SS guards watched close by.

"Emma, who are these people?" I asked.

"I'm not sure, but I heard from Pierre that they are Jewish, or political prisoners, and they are from concentration camps."

"What's a concentration camp?"

"Well, I'm not sure either, but Pierre told me that it had to do with Jews and political prisoners."

"You and Pierre better be careful." I pointed at the men below us. "Emma, I don't want to visit you down there."

"I think we are safe. Our Party and camp inspectors have other worries now than checking what I do."

The beautiful spring days of March could not lessen the chaos and the desperation that was now common within the Bavarian villages and towns not yet taken by the enemy. Emma and I spent our duty-free time searching for stores which still could supply food. We carried our rations and the half-filled pail of water past people who had nowhere to go. Yet, in all that chaos and nothingness, there was no looting; no one protested, and even during the pitch-dark blackouts, the "have-nots" did not accost the "haves." The homeless have-nots did what was expected of them: For hours, they stood or sat apathetically in line, until they received the second-hand clothing of people who had died in bombings.

I had my own pain. I had a cold, my ears ached and my tonsils were infected to a degree that my supervisor told me, "I'll replace you for the weekend, but be back by Monday if you can. You shouldn't go home, but I know you will anyway."

Friday night I arrived in Wiesau, feverish and aching. Cousin Joey was waiting with his bike. "Hop on the back," he directed. "I'll get you home."

Mama was waiting with hot salt water. She made me gargle, she rubbed my neck and back with warm grease, and she brought me a cup of goat's milk. I slept soundly for the first time in days, and her home remedies had me feeling better by Sunday morning. It was so good to be home, and I longed to stay.

Mama did most of the talking. "I think I know why Papa failed the test," she told me. "Knowing him, he couldn't report or return stragglers and soldiers who probably, without it being their fault, were AWOL. The way times are, who knows what would happen after they are returned to their units. I don't think your Papa wanted to turn them in and become responsible for their fate. As far as I know, your Papa has never failed a test when he made up his mind to pass it."

Now I understood. Mama talked about Uncle Pepp and Cousin Karl, and the rift that existed within the family. "I stay out of it," Mama said. "I like Pepp, and I like Karl. As for Ida — well that's Ida. You must go and say good-bye to Pepp, though. He always asks about you."

As I arrived at the bakery, Aunt Nannie said, "Why, Anneliese, you are feeling better, I see. If you are looking for Pepp, he is in his office. He'll see you."

I knocked softly. Uncle Pepp opened the door and motioned to the big chair. "What can I do for you?"

"Nothing. I came to say good-bye."

"So good-bye it is," Uncle Pepp mumbled.

His voice and his demeanor startled me. "If you are busy, I'll leave."

"No," he pointed at the chair again. "You just sit there, and I'll tell you when you can leave."

Resting his chin in his hands, he looked at me, pondering. "Everybody comes and tells me, 'I'm leaving.' So you'll leave too. You should be home with your mother, but you are out there, getting bombed and shot at just like the men." His gaze went past me. "They went, but most of them didn't come back. The ones who came home are crippled for life in one way or another. Tell me, for what?"

He nodded. "Oh, yes, for the 1000 Year Reich. What a Reich it is. It started with a few crazy men and they've led and lied until everyone followed into abysmal destruction of humanity. We hollered and screamed and went with them; now, we drown in our own blood. How they have changed us."

"Uncle . . ." He didn't hear me, and I didn't dare to move as he went on. "They didn't change us, we did that ourselves. Now, I expect, they'll hold everyone accountable." He shook his head. "All my life I tried to do right. Then, in one minute, I ruined it all. Just because Karl joined the party and didn't tell me, I pushed him into this damn war. Now he is in France, doing God knows what? Killing, fighting, or running to save himself. He shouldn't have joined the Nazi party without telling me . . . and I should have signed. Now, nothing is the same. He and I have changed."

I had never seen Uncle Pepp like this. I got up and gingerly put my hand on his shoulder. "It wasn't your fault! It's the war," I said. "They would have taken Karl anyway. Everybody has to go to war. I bet after this one there won't be any more wars, because there isn't anyone left to fight."

He laughed bitterly. "You would think so. We learn a lot in a lifetime, but no one in the world learns about keeping peace. Every time there is a war, they say it is for some cause, and then it will bring peace forever. The human race is the dumbest species there is. For thousands of years legions of people have fought and maimed each other for one cause or another. They took land from their so-called enemy. When you look around, you see that years later they gave it back. Never mind the corpses underneath the land ... the young were told to conquer."

Uncle Pepp's eyes bored into mine. "You think this war is the last war? Anneliese, don't mind my laughing. Some day you may have a son who will get his draft notice to fight in another war . . . again, they'll promise you, 'This is the last of all wars.' On the other side there will be a mother who will have to send her son for the same reason. To stop war!

"What we have not yet learned is the simple truth: Wars lay the seeds and breed another more horrible war than the ones before."

Uncle Pepp came close to me. "I always told Max you should have been his first born son, but I'm glad you're not. Maybe you will make it through this war. You will, if you're lucky and have a say about it." He kissed me on the forehead. "Now go, and do come back, you hear me!"

He walked away from me and sighed. "Tell your mama, Mrs. Beer heard last night that Otto died of his wounds in Russia. It's not official, but a soldier, who was lucky enough to be transferred out, sent word to them. That's her second son who didn't make it home." He waved, walked out and shut the door quietly.

I sat still, thinking about what I had just heard. My heart ached for Uncle Pepp because I knew he hurt, but I knew there wasn't anything anyone could do about it. Just like the war going on all around us, I thought. We couldn't do anything about that either, because if you did, you were shot anyway.

On the way home Uncle Pepp's revelations were still on my mind. It bothered me how helpless we were, and I thought of Papa and his pebble story. Searching the sides of the road, I collected pebbles until several lay in my cupped hand. Just like Papa had said, there were no two alike. Selecting all the while, I threw several as far as I could, until it came down to one smooth pebble, oval, with its edges uneven. The rough, bluish-black pebble became my own. Lodged deeply within my pocket, it made me feel better, and I wished that Papa could be here and, as he had done so often, set everything right.

After dinner, Mama walked to Wiesau with me, and she waited until the train left. I sat by the window, and the brightness of the Sunday afternoon mocked what went on along the way. People were on the move coming to, or leaving towns, while at the same time, columns of our soldiers marched behind their officers in military vehicles.

Pointing at the soldiers, someone said, "Thank God, they are going in the other direction. I hope they stay away from this train, I have been shot at enough."

At Schwandorf, rail cars filled with children who were part of the Kinder Land Verschickung, or Child Land Placement (KLV)[1], were across from us. These children, grade schoolers, were packed in, sardine fashion.   Some stretched their skinny arms out the windows reaching for morsels of food or the touch of a hand. Several soldiers waited on the platform and we watched as they touched as many hands as they could. The soldiers shook their heads, and hands moved across their brows and eyes.   We, in our coach, watched and waved, while some passengers wondered aloud, "Where are these children coming from? Where are they going?"

Silently, I wondered if they would ever see their mamas, their families, or their homes again. We reached Regensburg, and on Monday morning I went back to work. More than ever, regular schedules were no more. Work, air raids, sleep, search for food and exhaustion became intermingled. I rarely saw the Lehnerts. They, too, suffered: their three-year-old grandson, Gerhard, died of pneumonia. Mr. Lehnert bemoaned the lack of medication and early treatment, which took the little one's life.

Emma said that Pierre spoke of going home after the war, and he had asked her to come with him.

"Are you leaving Germany to live in France?"

"No, Anneliese, I took enough risks here. Every time I saw Pierre it was connected to a certain risk. I knew you would never tell. But what would have happened if someone would have turned me in? We love each other, but going to France would be taking the greatest risk of all. Even Pierre couldn't deny that most French people hate all Germans, collectively. Can you imagine what they would do to me? I'm not going with Pierre. Once he leaves, we won't see each other again."

I turned toward Emma. "You don't see it that way, but I think that Pierre took advantage of you," I said. "It must have brought him

---

[1] Kinder Land Verschickung. In order to preserve and propagate the German race, youth from large cities, which were often bombed, were removed from their homes during the war. They were transported to southern Germany where bombings were uncommon. Since the parents remained in the large cities, a great number of these young people were orphans by the time the war ended. After the war, Germany had no social agency to look after these displaced young people. In order to survive they banded together to beg or steal, and sometimes they even prostituted themselves for food or lodging.

satisfaction . . . getting even. I bet he said, 'I'm a forced labor worker. I have syphilis. While in Germany, I will infect whomever I can.' He is the lowest of the low! There, now I said it!"

"Why, Anneliese. You hate him. You hate the French!"

"No, Papa said that I shouldn't hate, but I surely dislike him a great deal. Tell me, when did he ever think of you? He let you risk your life! Is that love? You tell me."

"It will be out of my hands soon," Emma said. "Let's hope the Americans get here before the Russians do."

"I'm not waiting around for either one. I'll just go home, one day soon."

Now I had revealed what I had been thinking about ever since I had come back. Before the enemy came, I wanted to be with Mama and my family. I was afraid of being stuck in some rail car like the KLV children.

"Emma, when the Americans are nearing Erfurt, or Schweinfurt, I'm out of here. If you want to wait until you are cut off from your family, fine, but I want to be with mine."

Mr. Lehnert listened quietly when I told him what I had planned. "Anneliese, pack your belongings and I'll mail them for you. We'll trust they will arrive at your home. Should you have to walk, baggage would be too cumbersome." It didn't take me long to pack and Mr. Lehnert kept his word.

Two blouses, one skirt, a heavy coat, a scarf, and my shoes were all the baggage I had when I decided to take off without permission. Mr. Lehnert was right; we couldn't use the railroad since the platforms were filled with military units and refugees being stuck, going nowhere.

Emma wanted to stay with Pierre, so she backed out at the last minute; fortunately Maria, who lived in Weiden, decided to walk home too.

Before the night shift, I said goodby. "Anneliese, trust your gut feeling and be wary," Mr. Lehnert advised. "You have ninety miles ahead of you and that can be a difficult journey, so you and your friend stay together, no matter what. Sleep out in the open because barns burn so easily. Oh, yes, should anyone come and ask for your whereabouts, we'll tell them that we don't know where you are. You left for the night shift. That's all we know."

I handed Mr. Lehnert my rent money, and he pushed it back. "No, pay us some other time. You may need it, so hide it on your body and don't let anyone see it." Wordlessly, I hugged Mr. Lehnert.

Mrs. Lehnert stepped up and hugged me tightly. "We loved having you," she said. She handed me a small package. "Hide these two slices of bread under your blouse. Even if they get hard, don't eat them until you see your town." She stepped away from me. "Anneliese, should you change your mind after your night shift, just come back. You can stay with us as long as you want. We'll worry about you, so let us know how you fared." She crossed my forehead, and sprinkled me with Holy Water.

I couldn't stand it anymore. Grabbing my sweater, I ran out of the apartment that had been my second home. Maria and I put in a blurred night shift, and at seven in the morning we set out on our trek home. We were apprehensive: Masses, pulling small wagons or carts, streamed into Regensburg. But we mixed in with others, who, like us, were walking toward the frontlines. Silently, I thanked Mr. Lehnert for his advise. Without baggage, Maria and I could move unencumbered; for a while, we and several others had a ride on a farmer's wagon. As his ox-team moved slowly toward Regenstauf, we dozed intermittently. Before Regenstauf, the farmer told everyone, "That's as far as I go. Everybody off."

We walked, begged for rides, and by the end of the first day we had made nearly twenty miles. We stayed with several women and their children, and we laid on the hard ground, huddling closely, dozing.

We hungered until we could buy some rations and we walked on, begged for rides, and slept in farm yards, until we were near Schwandorf. Conditions in Schwandorf were chaotic. We walked in fields and ditches because the roads were taken over by a mixture of humanity. Maria and I passed Croatians, SS groups from Hungary, forced labor workers from Poland, France, Russia and Spain. Even though we were a group, we were glad that our soldiers were near because we feared for our safety. We were tired, but we pushed on. We wanted to get away from Schwandorf so for several miles we kept to the side roads. By now we had formed a bond with the people who walked with us. We wanted to survive, and we found that looking out for each other ensured a greater margin of safety. We spent another night in the open somewhere near Schwandorf when gun fire roused us. Planes were circling several military vehicles, soldiers ran for ditches, and we did the same.

A soldier near us called out, "Take the woods and walkways. You'll make greater progress away from us."

But even there, we moved at a snail's pace. Sharing duties, we stopped in towns. Some bought food rations, while others searched for safe drinking water. After sleeping outdoors near villages and walking through woods and fields, we reached Weiden, Maria's hometown. She skipped, ran and cried out, "While we walked I didn't dare to hope. Now that I'm home, I don't care what happens." She turned toward us. "I hope you'll make it too." And she was gone.

I criss-crossed through streets and joined a group heading toward Wiesau. A little girl grasped my hand while her Mama pulled a small hand wagon filled with boxes and a toddler who hung onto the sides. They turned off near Reuth, hoping relatives could take them in. Groups became fewer in numbers as we walked on to the proximity of the front. We stopped at outlying farms and asked how far the enemy soldiers had advanced. No one knew for sure, but we learned that American troops were near Nuremberg, and the Russian soldiers were advancing toward the Sudetenland. We slept in the woods, and early in the morning a wave of hope took hold of us when we heard that the American President Roosevelt had died. Maybe now peace would come. Eagerly, I pushed on, hoping to make it home before the enemy overtook us.

Avoiding Wiesau, I was glad that the pathway through the woods was familiar to me. Once in a while, I could hear the humming of the metal ravens as they circled back and forth. By now I had grown accustomed to their frequent presence and I kept walking until I saw the foreign labor workers' barracks. In the distance, straight ahead, stood our home. Ignoring everything around me, I ran, until I reached our garden gate.

Resi was in the garden, and she cried out, "Anneliese, where did you come from? Mama is so worried. The Postmaster, Mr. Roth, himself came to inquire about your whereabouts. Mama told him she had no idea and as far as she knew you were in Regensburg. I am so glad you're safe."

I took the steps to the entry in twos and rang the bell. Mama opened the door and just stood there. "Oh my God, thank you, thank you, she is safe." She grabbed me, shook and hugged me simultaneously. "Anneliese, how can you worry me so! I didn't sleep, after Mr. Roth came. Then Mr. Lehnert finally got through. I didn't know if it was better or worse knowing you were on your way home. No one knew where you were."

"Mama, I wanted to come home before the front line made it impossible. I want to be here with you," I cried out.

"I'm angry with you for just thinking of yourself and what you want, but I am so glad you made it home," Mama said. "Neither of the situations would have been good. I am alone in the house since Mrs. Dimpfl left a few days ago. She hopes that the American troops will take Hof since that is a much better fate than being within the Russian front line. She told me, 'Peppi, we have nothing. But I hope that even though my parents and my sister are displaced too, we can stay with them for a while. I'm sure when Hans comes home from the war, that's where he will hope to find us.'" Mama sighed. "She was a stranger when she came, but we became friends and we helped each other. I will miss her."

"Mama, I hope she made it. The roads and everything is horrible out there. So many people have no place to go."

Mama looked at me and held her nose. "Anneliese," she said, "I'll fetch some water from the rain barrel, so you can wash yourself. You and your clothes need it, and you look beaten. You need sleep."

Resi, Max, and Irmgard crowded around me, and Max complained, "She can walk home from Regensburg, and I can't even go to the football field without permission. That's not fair."

"Fair or not," Mama said, "everyone will do as I say. We must get rested up for whatever is ahead of us."

I could see that Mama was happy that I was home, and within a day the forces of war encircled us from all sides. We fearfully wondered who would reach us first, the Russian Army or the Americans? We were praying for the coming of the American forces as night fell.

CHAPTER TWENTY

WAR'S END — 1945

<u>Monday, April 16, 1945</u>

New, unfamiliar noises had kept us awake all night. Now, as dawn was breaking we opened the kitchen windows and watched anxiously as huge tanks and smaller military vehicles raced up and down the road while a constant stream of weary foot soldiers moved through our town. Our soldiers tersely called out to each other whenever vehicles slowed down, and they carried their rifles pointed forward for action.

Max burst barefooted into the kitchen. "Mama, did you see all these soldiers? I am going outside. I want to look at those tanks and watch how they steer them."

"You will do no such thing," Mama snapped. "You'll stay right here with us and from now on, I must know where you are at all times. Whatever we do today, we will do it together. Is that understood?"

"Yes, Mama. We won't leave," Resi said.

"Max, you may sit by the window and make sure that you stay out of the way," Mama commanded.

Max's shrill cry demanded our attention, "Look! Look, Mama! Just look at those people! Where do they come from?"

We joined Max at the window and unbelieving, we watched. Soldiers and old men with their rifles drawn encircled column after column of walking, emaciated men and women of all ages, clad in gray and blue-striped prison garb. Every head was clean shaven, their dull eyes were unusually large in sunken sockets, and their pallid skin stretched over the protruding bones of their faces. The more able prisoners shuffled and limped along while some comrades carried those unable to walk. It seemed no one wanted to stay behind, and when others tried to lean on someone, they were pushed aside. As several marchers fell, those who followed closed ranks and walked over or around the silent forms.

Horror-stricken by the scene below, we watched. Suddenly, the whole column sent out an eerie wail. The surprised soldiers and guards were taken unaware and they stood momentarily still as the prisoners broke away and staggered toward the five houses on our street. A great tide of marchers pushed and pitched themselves against our garden gate until the hinges gave and the gate fell. Trampling over the gate, they swarmed into the yard below us, pleading, "Water! Water!" Others stretched out their stick-like arms and called, "Bread, bread."

Some had left the group and they tore out the chives, parsley, and anything green that had started to sprout in Mama's herb garden. Mama walked away from the window, came back, and threw our few slices of bread into the outstretched arms of the men and women. The skeletal bodies below us groveled and fought each other for the morsels of bread. Several women cried out like children as they emptied our rain barrel and curbed their thirst.

The soldiers and guards cursed and threatened Mama, "You stupid woman," a soldier shouted angrily, "close the windows immediately and don't you open them again until the roads are clear. You should be shot for causing this!"

Even through the closed windows we heard clubs and gun barrels crack down on the hunger-crazed marchers. Screams, wails, and shouts intermingled with a guard's command: "Back in line! Get back in line! Move on, you bitch, or I will shoot you."

We shook with fear as we glanced out through the closed windows. Running from room to room, we peaked through the curtains and watched as the human columns of misery inched their way toward the hills until they entered the forest. As soon as the last row disappeared from view, we opened the windows for fresh air, but nothing could sweep away the horrific scenes we had just witnessed.

"Who were these people?" Mama asked. "Where did they come from?"

"I don't know," I replied, "but I saw people clad in such suits working in Regensburg after bombings. They were repairing bombed out bridges as we were routed around them. I asked Emma where these people came from, and she said that they were imprisoned in concentration camps where Jews and political prisoners were sent to pay for crimes against the Fatherland. She heard that one such camp was located in our area by Flossenburg, while another concentration camp was closer to Regensburg and Munich, near Dachau."

Mama shook her head. "I wonder if those marchers were prisoners that came from Flossenburg?"

We were still trying to sort out what we had witnessed when Max said, "Sh." He counted, "One ... two ... three ... four ... five." Five shots had pierced the air. We shuddered, and Max clung to Mama and asked, "They didn't shoot those people, did they?"

Mama looked at me, laid her fingers on her lips, and reassured Max, "No, Max, I don't think they would."

I shut my eyes, but I could not rid my mind of the images of the five victims. Mama sighed. "Anneliese, we will stay together, no matter what the next few days bring. We will get through this, day by day."

Since Mama had given our bread ration away during the morning, we stilled our hunger with dried mushrooms and blueberries that had come from the woods around us. Throughout the morning and into the early afternoon, we watched with apprehension and fear as bands of refugees pulled their hand wagons filled with their few belongings past our home. Small children sat atop the wagons, others were carried by adults who walked alongside.

By now, most roads were closed because our military vehicles and soldiers moved back and forth on main roads and highways. Fields and meadows, their new green spears trampled under, had become walk paths for hundreds of refugees as they searched for unknown, safe destinations.

Mama and I sat by the kitchen table. "Mama, will we leave the house and get away?" I asked.

"No," she said, and she retrieved a letter from a drawer. "Papa wrote this letter well over a year ago. Even then, he must have guessed at what was coming. I didn't want to worry you way back then, but now it is time to make a decision. Here, read it, and then tell me what you think".

Blein Mellin, February 20, 1944

My Dearest Peppi,

Finally, I am able to write. By now, you should have
the card I wrote on February fifteenth. So far I am well
and I hope that all of you are well also. Lately, I have
traveled much and, up to now, I had the good fortune
to escape the fate of war. We were to go from
Schneidemuehl to Neustettin, but a blizzard isolated
us and we were confined to the Schneidemuehl area
for two days and nights. During this time, our whole
battalion, two companies and all our staff officers,
were captured by the Russians. We never learned how
many of our troops died fighting or how great a
number was taken as prisoners of war. It was by
chance that we escaped the iron circle the Russians
had around our fighting troops. The situation changes
daily; we are always traveling on the run. Presently,
we are near the town of Dranburg. I know you can find
it on the map.

To live, that is, to eat, we have more than enough. All
the towns and villages around us are depeopled. The
livestock in the barns is bellowing for fodder, but there
is no one to attend to its needs.

Peppi, this pales in comparison to the suffering of the
civilian population we witness each day. The
suffering war brings to anyone's home territory is
indescribable. I cannot write and describe sufficiently
what takes place on the streets once you become a
refugee. If our home area is destined to fall to the
enemy, please, Peppi, stay where you are! Please, do
NOT take the children on the streets! Many homeless
have perished there. It is a heartless, nomadic life. It
is devastating. Even if the enemy takes our

hometown, stay at home, don't leave, believe me it is the best choice under the circumstances. Peppi, don't despair. Even though the situation is most serious, we will see each other again.

If I stay well, I will search for opportunities and I will come home to you. You can be sure of that! My letter speaks of most serious topics, but I don't want to paint beautiful pictures for you. I give you realities. How is Anneliese in Regensburg? Is she well? What is new at home? I long for a letter from you, but I know the mail situation is not your fault. How is Resi, Max and Irmgard?

Now, my dear, I wish you everything good. I pray that you and the children are well. Hoping that we will see each other soon at home, I greet and kiss you and the children. My heart belongs to all of you.

Your Max.

"Papa wants us to stay home, so we stay," I said.

"I worry, Anneliese. I don't think Papa saw prisoners from the concentration camps or the foreign laborers forced to work in the factories near us. I wonder if he heard and saw what the Russians do to women and children? What will we do if these people come to our homes?"

"Has Resi read Papa's letter?" I asked.

"No, but she will. She should be part of any decision we make within the next few days. Look, she has fallen asleep next to Irmgard. Let her sleep. Who knows what the next few hours and days will bring?"

We quickly became accustomed to the new noises and the stream of destitute homeless. Our garden gate had been broken by starving, oppressed prisoners, but they had not entered our home. We locked our doors, and we stayed inside.

<u>Tuesday, April 17, 1945</u>

Mama got up early and went directly to the herb garden. She was concerned that it could be a complete loss since the new sprouts of herbs had been torn out by their roots. The rain barrel was still empty, which meant no washing clothes for another day.

Anni came by. "Peppi, the grocery stores are selling their stored staples and they are not asking for food stamps. We must go to town and get what we can."

"Anneliese," Mama said, "you go with Anni, and Resi must go for our rations of milk and bread. Hurry now. I stay with Max and Irmgard, and we keep everything safe."

"There is time yet, Peppi," Anni continued, "Anneliese, make sure you bring your ID card. You will need proof that your family is in residence. Otherwise you won't get anything."

Avoiding the highways, we cautiously surged ahead on paths the refugees had trampled down when they crossed the fields and meadows. We approached the store and joined the seemingly endless line of those waiting. Several women were talking about the war.

A woman asked, "Mary, did you hear about the shooting yesterday?"

"Yes, I heard, but did it actually happen? Why on earth would someone shoot another person without reason? It doesn't make sense."

"It's the war, nothing makes sense in a war," another woman added. She turned to a woman near her, "Mrs. Wicker, your husband is a big shot in the party, what does he say now? What happens when the Russians or Americans come knocking at your door?"

"When that happens, we know what we have to do. We have pledged that we will not be serfs to the Russians or Americans. We have our means. Mark my words, though, the war isn't over yet."

"Can you believe that?" Anni asked as she turned and called out, "Take off your blinders, woman! When will you see the truth? The war is over!"

A wailing air raid siren brought everyone up short, yet each remained rigidly frozen to her spot in the line. The small, dark spots in the sky changed shape as they moved downward until they buzzed over us. Suddenly, bullets whizzed past us as the American fighter planes flew unopposed over the city. We coiled up, pressed against each other, and stood our ground.

The fighter planes above us meant business. They flew back and forth, they circled, and at uneven intervals, they shot at targets that I could not see. German military vehicles sped past us, and they returned the planes' fire, but they were no match for the enemy above. Several people in the waiting group prayed, but all the while, everyone stood firm and continued to inch toward the grocery store.

Finally, after what seemed hours of waiting, Anni and I entered the store. The grocer announced, "I am impartial and fair. Five small bags are on the counter. Five of you come forward, take the bag closest to you, and do not hold up the line and do not open your bag until you leave the store. Remember, every bag has the same contents, and I won't make any exchanges."

Anni and I each took a bag and left quickly. Once outside, I opened my bag and looked.

"Anni, I have a fourth pound of butter and two packages of pudding."

"Great," Anni said. "I have the same. Just tell me, where we can get enough milk to cook the pudding?"

She slumped to the ground and cried hysterically, "No meat, no bread, no milk. I got shot at, and what do I have? Just smell that stinking, rancid butter!"

I put everything back into my bag and cried out, "I will not look at it and I will not smell it! Mama sent me to stand in line and then I come back with this. I didn't move when the planes shot at us. What more could I do?"

Military vehicles streamed into town. Even the side roads were momentarily off limits because the vehicles brought wounded soldiers to the market square. Laid out on stretchers, the seriously wounded were placed in the shadow of the trees which surrounded the church. Others, on crutches, wobbled in unsteadily and searched until they secured a resting place. Father Neidl moved among the soldiers. "War has come to our town." he said. He gave the Last Rites to the dying and prayed for their everlasting peace.

The American planes returned. Circling over the market square, they shot down at will. We hurried past the wounded soldiers and zig-zagged home through the fields and ditches.

Mama had waited anxiously. "What took so long? I saw the planes and I was worried sick about you! Did you take cover?"

"No, Anni and I held our place in line, and we just ducked when we heard the bullets whizzing by."

"For this you stand in line and risk your life? Anneliese, you are eighteen years old. Sometimes I think Resi at fourteen shows more sense than you do."

"Mama, you can take the rancid butter back if you want to or just throw it out the window. You should have sent Resi, then she would finally know what it is like to be shot at."

With that I stomped out of the kitchen, slammed the door as hard as I could and ran outside. I threw myself down and pounded my fists on the ground until they hurt. All the while, I cried in frustration.

Wednesday, April 18, 1945

We lived a nightmare. We slept when we could no longer go on and we gave our minds over to a stupor that shut out fear and anguish over the horror that might start at any moment. When I awoke from a troubled sleep, I left my bed and entered the kitchen. Mama had been up most of the night. Her stomach pains denied her sleep and the arthritic leg pains forced her to walk through the kitchen and the hallway most of the night.

"I couldn't sleep, so I kindled a fire in the stove. I heard soldiers move through the city."

"Yes, Mama, I heard them, too. They must be in the woods and they must have us surrounded by now. How will we get to town for our milk and rations?"

Before Mama could answer, we heard someone move the makeshift gate. Apprehensively, Mama went to the window. "It is Pepp. Let him in."

He came up the steps two at a time and walked straight to the kitchen. "Pepp, what is it? What is going on?"

"I thought I should check with you before all hell breaks loose out there. Twice, I was stopped for an ID check. Both times, the officers in charge asked me why I wasn't on the front. 'What front?' I wanted to ask them. Well, when they saw I was the town's baker, they let me through. Earlier this morning I spoke with Father Neidl. He thinks we have but two or three days before the Americans or Russians will move and take the town. Let us hope it will be the Americans. Right now, our Army is rounding up fifteen-year-old boys and taking them to the front surrounding the city. I wonder how heroic these older men must feel leading young boys, like lambs, to slaughter." Uncle Pepp shook his head. "I just saw the Huebner boy, the Schicker boy, and several others walk off with an officer toward the Waldsassen-Eger area. They are barely fifteen. What a waste. What a waste!"

Uncle Pepp lowered his face into his hands and shook his head. "When will we learn not to waste our young people for wars? The young and the women never start wars. No, it is the old men. They train the young until they are ready to kill. Instead of making war, they should be out playing soccer. They should be learning a trade and they should be thinking of girls. But we have taken all this from them in the name of patriotism. What we do is maim them or offer them premature death instead of peace and freedom." Looking glassy-eyed and dazed, he wiped his brow. "I must be going nuts!" he said. "Peppi, the whole world is nuts. Now we will see what the glory of war is all about. You, women and children will have to fend for yourselves. You are welcome to stay with us at the bakery, but you would have to sleep on the floor. The barn is already filled with refugees, but we will manage."

"Thank you, Pepp, but Max asked me to keep the family together and stay at home."

"Are your sure? Remember, you have children."

"We will manage."

"I must get back to the bakery. If possible, I will come back again. If not, may God watch over you." He reached under his jacket. "I brought bread so you won't have to face the crowd at the bakery."

Mama held the bread up and inhaled the fresh-baked aroma. Tears welled up. "Only your bread smells like this, Pepp. There is no other bread like it."

"That is true" Uncle Pepp said, smiling with pride. He put on his visored cap, lifted his hand, and waved. "You, Anneliese and Resi, you help your mother and take care of the two little ones. It is good that they can sleep, yet. Take care of each other, I may not be able to return. Only God knows what is in store." He gave a brief wave and then left.

When Resi, Max, and Irmgard awoke, we savored a slice of Uncle Pepp's freshly baked bread. The little ones drank a cup of milk and Mama, Resi, and I drank warm water flavored with dried berries.

"I want everyone's help," Mama directed shortly after. "Lay out your clothes in case we need to pack in a hurry. I will check what food rations we can manage. For the next few days, you will ask my permission if you want to go outside. Remember, I need to know where you are at all times. I don't think there are any more rations in the stores uptown. If there is, Anni or someone will know. We must listen to the radio, get things in order, so we can stay together."

Thursday, April 19, 1945

Anni came to check on us. "The stores are out of food, workers have abandoned the fields, and the factories have bolted their doors," she said. "The only local news we get is what we might hear from a neighbor."

Max kept himself busy looking out the window. "Anni, here comes your sister, Marie," he called.

"Peppi! Peppi, let me in." Glad to see someone new, I met her in the foyer.

She rushed past me, into the kitchen, then she turned and faced us. "The Army Field Police caught a young soldier," she blurted out. "Since he left the front line, he's in jail for deserting, waiting for a trial."

Mama turned ghastly pale. "How can they arrest a soldier now! Where would he desert to when all of Germany is a front line?"

"No, Peppi. Not deserting," Marie said. "He is accused of cowardice before the enemy. Five people were picked as jurors, and if they find him guilty, they will hang him for sure."

Max's eyes flashed wild, and he was breathing hard. "Mama," he cried, "Who hangs our soldiers?"

"Max, don't get ahead of yourself." Mama assured him, "So far, no one is hanging anyone."

It was quiet for but a moment, then shots rang out in the distance. The grisly image of five gaunt bodies flashed through my mind and again, I felt the fear of bullets whizzing by. Slowly the realization set in: soldiers kill others for little or no reason. I started to shake. Tomorrow, or the next day, we could die.

The afternoon hours dragged on. We watched as American planes broke through the clouds and droned down, firing at anyone who came into view. Finally, the sirens blew and we rushed to the basement.

"When we get back upstairs, gather up your pillows and blankets," Mama said. "We will spend the night down here. It will be safer for us."

Irmgard fussed. She was covered from head to foot with impetigo, a contagious skin disease usually caused by bacteria. The eruptions, especially on her face, were painful, and she was hungry.

I felt secure in the basement, yet so alone, and wished for the comfort and strength of the woman I had met in the Munich bomb shelter. I went to Resi and Max and held them close to me, comforting them while I trembled.

"Anneliese," Mama asked, "are you cold?"

"Yes, Mama," I lied. I did not want for her to know that fear made me tremble — as I remembered the shelter in Munich.

A long time passed before we heard the "All Clear" signal. We struggled out of the basement drained and weary. The sounds of attack subsided and the momentary stillness stretched our nerves to the breaking point.

"Mama, I don't like it in the basement," Max protested.

Irmgard joined right in. "It's cold and dark down there. I want to stay up here with Max."

"Well, we could stay upstairs, "Mama said. "At least we can hear what is taking place and see what is coming. If we do stay upstairs Resi, Anneliese, one of us will stay awake and watch at all times. The worst is that I cannot advise you what to watch for."

Outside, a great commotion arose so Mama turned the lock on the window. Someone shouted, "They hung him! Oh, my God in heaven, they hung him."

Mama frantically opened the window wide, and shouted back, "Who was hanged?"

The stranger continued, "I saw it, but I cannot believe it! They hanged that young soldier. Go see! Right now he is hanging from one of the trees near the town hall. I heard several people beg him to say that he was confused, that he was sorry, but he said, 'I am not going back to the front nor will I fight anymore.' They took him out, put a black cloth over his head, and hung him right there! The young man jerked once or twice and then it was over." The stranger turned sideways. He retched and vomited until weakness caused him to stagger and he sat down.

People who had listened stood silent. Someone helped the man struggle to his feet and he walked onto the fields and disappeared into the distance.

Mama closed the window. "I won't open that window, again, not tonight, come what may," Mama said. She continued to look out. She had a grim, troubled look on her face, but she kept silent.

That night Resi and I took turns sleeping and keeping watch. At first, we slept in intervals and then, not at all. We watched from the window and tried to catch a glimpse of something, anything, in the black-out darkness.

"Anneliese, look. There are tanks and soldiers down there. Are you sure these are ours?"

"Of course, Resi. If they were the enemy's tanks, the soldiers would stop here to check the houses along the road. Besides, I don't hear any shooting. You hear that first."

We kept watch until an uneasy sleep overtook us both. Max came in from his bedroom and shook me. "Wake up! Anneliese, if Mama caught you sleeping, you'd be in trouble. I think you should wake her up. Look at those big guns!"

Huge artillery guns moved along the street, then on through the fields, and finally up to the hills by Konnersreuth, a nearby farm village. I went to my room and looked out the window. Planes and guns encircled Fuchsmuehl, but where were the church steeples? Were they hidden by low-lying clouds, or billowing masses of dust and smoke? My heart pounded wildly as I wondered, what fate awaited us?

"Wake Irmgard," Mama called out. "All of you get dressed. Make sure you dress warmly. We may have to hide in the basement or leave home in a hurry, so we must be ready."

Like prisoners in our own home, we watched uneasily as neighbors and strangers pushed their hand wagons across the fields. Anni came by.

"Peppi, I know you are determined to stay here, but we are leaving for Dobrigau. Some time ago Mister Miller said he would take us in. Should we ask him to keep room for you, too?"

"No, Anni, Max asked us to stay home so we will stay. Do you think it will be better at the Miller's farm?"

"Not better, but safer. If those big guns start shooting, nothing will be safe. I have to go, Mama is waiting."

Anni hugged each of us and then hugged Mama. Tears welled up in my eyes as Mama said, "Anni, I hope I made the right decision, and I am doing what is best for the children's safety. Max asked me in a letter to stay home and keep them safe. God be with us."

I kept hearing Anni's heart-rending sobs long after she left. We remained quiet; we listened and watched while time passed by slowly. Our quiet erupted into frenzied tension as bombs or shells exploded in the distance. The fear of war in our town gripped us. Barely a hundred feet from our home, our soldiers strung barricades of barbed wire and put cement pillars in place to stop invading tanks. Meanwhile Army trucks backed artillery guns into position right behind the barricades. The movement of troops and equipment and the noises of war came menacingly close. The thought of another night's black-out in the basement, and the presence of the enemy all around us, broke Mama's confidence.

CHAPTER TWENTY-ONE

RUNNING FROM THE ENEMY

"Anneliese, Resi, help Max and Irmgard," she called out. "Go! Put on several layers of underwear and wear as many of your clothes as you can. Take blankets. I will fetch what remains of our rations. Hurry! We must leave this instant." She turned toward me. "You check all the windows and doors, and make sure they are locked. Max, you will feed the chickens, goats and the rabbits, and I will quickly take their milk. Bring the hand wagon to the garden gate and we will place Irmgard in the wagon. When we are ready, you and Resi will pull, and Max and I will push."

While Resi took care of Irmgard, I helped Max feed the animals. As we readied ourselves, Max quietly put on everything I laid out. "Wear enough clothing," I told him, "but be sure you can walk or run if we need to. I will be back as soon as I am dressed."

We rejoined Mama. "I hope we can make it to Dobrigau," she said. "Now, no matter what, unless I say otherwise, we will stay together. I hope and pray we will be safe."

Mama dipped her fingers in the stoup of holy water and made the sign of the cross on our foreheads. "In the name of the Father, the Son, and the Holy Ghost," she prayed, "may we be safe. Now, everyone, do as I said. Resi, come help with the wagon."

In a frenzy, we left our home. Resi and I picked up the handle and pulled the wagon through the garden gate. Once out in the street, we turned and became part of the rumbling masses going to somewhere unknown, to do we knew not what.

Mama called from the back, "Anneliese, go through the market square. It will be quicker and we will check if anyone has more recent news than we have."

The wagon bumped and rocked along on the worn cobblestones as Resi and I pulled in silence until we came upon the market square. I suddenly dropped the handle of the wagon. I shrank back and screamed,"Mama! Oh, Mama, look!"

Mama and Max came around the wagon and stood horror struck. There, on a lower limb of a tall chestnut tree, hung the young soldier. Near him, we saw the wounded and we heard helpless and dying soldiers crying out in pain.

"Mama, I can't go past him! I just can't!"

"Anneliese, we must. Don't look at him," Mama urged, "just go on as fast as you can."

Hypnotized, Resi and I stood rooted to the ground, and we kept our eyes fixed on the ill-clad corpse. The rope, almost as thick as Max's arm, extended down and around the soldier's neck. His head, slumped forward and slightly to the side, rested on the lapel of his coat. The grotesque expression on his face revealed the frantic struggle to survive with but one more breath. His arms and hands hung limply at his sides. The front of his shabby coat was hidden by a huge, crude cardboard sign. Big, black letters proclaimed, "**I AM A TRAITOR TO MY COUNTRY!**" Several passersby stopped, crossed their forehead, and prayed while others walked by and turned away with their heads bowed.

Mama crossed herself and urged, "We must go on, Anneliese. Go on, now!" Resi and I grabbed the crossbar and moved on. The few stragglers we did encounter were as unsure about the whereabouts of the enemy as we were.

"We have about four miles to go before we reach Dobrigau," Mama reasoned. "The Americans must be close. We must hurry."

Resi and I pulled harder, while Mama and Max pushed. Our muscles strained as we moved hurriedly up the hills and across the grass land until we reached the forest's edge. It looked safe enough, yet we were unsure of what we might meet within the forest. The gunshots northwest of us became more intense and suddenly a red glow engulfed the sky above Konnersreuth. Yellow tongues of flames licked up the sides of barns and farm houses. Instantaneously, huge billows of smoke rose and hid the fate of the village and its inhabitants. Gripped by mounting panic, we pushed with renewed determination until we reached Dobrigau.

I stopped, exhausted. "I can't go on any further. Where can we stay?"

"Wait while I inquire where we can find shelter. Anneliese, Resi, stay near Irmgard. Max, come with me."

We sat on the ground and rested our sore limbs against the wagon wheels until Mama returned. "There isn't any room in the farms along the main road," she said. "We need to strike out and go to the farms along the pathways."

Discouraged and frightened, Resi asked, "What will we do if we can't find shelter for the night?"

"We'll deal with that when we have to," Mama said.

"You should have listened to Papa."

"Anneliese," Mama reprimanded, "I need your help, not your crying. We are here, so we must make the best of it."

We pushed on as darkness began to fall. After several stops, Mama finally found a farmer who said, "It isn't the best barn to be in, but you won't be out in the open. Several other women with their children have already settled in, but there is enough room for you. Don't use any lanterns. Fire, you know. I guess we still need blackout. The way things look now, it won't be long before the Americans are running over my fields."

"How is it out there?" a shadowy figure asked.

"We heard the big guns near Konnersreuth," Mama recalled, "and shortly after when the burning started."

"I'll take anything as long as the Russians don't reach us first. We just can't run anymore. I will stay here until the war is over," a woman mumbled. Pointing ahead, she added, "There is enough space left over there."

Growing used to the semi-darkness, we spotted the empty space. Mama pushed the wagon into the hay.

"Now wrap yourselves tightly in your blankets," someone advised, "and get some sleep."

I seethed with anger over Mama's decision to leave home, but I remained silent. Mama was walking back and forth. I watched her as she opened the small barn door and looked out into the darkness. The woman across from us got up. She joined Mama and soon they were talking, sharing concerns. After a while, the woman closed the door and said, "A woman in your condition should get all the sleep she can. Go back and lie down. At least you will get some rest."

"How can I rest? There will be no peace nor any rest for a long time."

"That's why you need sleep now. We all do. Come, go back to your space," the woman said.

Mama returned and bedded down between Max and Irmgard. Soon the breathing and snoring sounds of sleepers lulled me to sleep.

April 20, 1945

I realized I had slept into the morning hours as a loud explosion woke me with a start. Resi whispered "Anneliese, I am scared. Planes are flying over us and Mitterteich."

Someone said, "That big boom must have been the dynamiting of a bridge."

Mama stood near the barn door with several women. They were all talking at once. "I am not going to run again. I am staying right here, come what may," a woman said. Mama nodded agreement.

Irmgard crawled onto my lap and clung to me, whimpering, "I am hungry, I want to go home. Anneliese, I don't like it here."

I tried to reassure her. "We will be all right, Irmgard. Just try to be quiet."

"Ah!" I shuddered. Within my clothing, something skittered down my forearm, onto my hand, and into the hay below. Another mouse followed, seeking refuge from the pursuing cats. The cows mooed, the odor of steaming cow dung penetrated my nostrils, and the air in the old barn was foul. I handed Irmgard to Resi.

"I can't stand it here," I shouted. " Irmgard wants to go home, I want to go home, and I am not staying here another minute!"

Mama looked startled. "Anneliese, you cannot leave. We are safe here. The Americans or Russians are out there! We must stay together, and we cannot return home."

"Oh, yes, we can," I retorted. "I am going and no one is going to stop me. Papa told us to stay home and I am going to be there, waiting for him."

"Anneliese, that is enough. You do as you are told, and you are staying," Mama said angrily. Determined, she grabbed my arm and moved me toward our space.

Hot with anger, I wrenched loose from her grip and whirled to face her. "You did not do what Papa said, so I am not doing what you say. I am leaving!"

Before Mama could grab me again, I ran and ran, ignoring the footsteps behind me. I ran out the open barn door, past the surprised farmer, and down the dirt road toward the village. The footsteps behind me did not subside. I finally turned to see who it was, and Resi cried out, "Anneliese, wait! I want to go home with you." Tears streamed down her cheeks as she came up beside me. "Where are you going ?"

"Resi, quit your crying. You should be with Mama."

"No, I want to go home, too."

"Then come on, let's go." Within minutes, we reached the prairie's edge and the forest came into view in the threatening distance. My body trembled and my teeth chattered as I thought about crossing the open grass land. We had to reach the forest. Once there, we could hide among the trees and seek cover.

I looked around. Smoke clouds drifted up as several fighter planes circled over nearby towns and villages while others searched the hills around us. We had to cross into the forest now.

I grabbed Resi's hand. "We must run for the woods!"

Resi tarried. "I am scared, wait and see," she pleaded.

"If you are not coming with me right now," I screamed at her, "I will leave you and you can go back to Mama."

"No! No, I'm coming with you."

We ran, looking straight ahead. When we had passed the half-way point, I heard shots whiz by us. I held Resi's hand in a vise grip, and we ran zig-zag until the edge of the woods came close, closer. My breath burned in my lungs with each gasping breath, and I felt as though my chest would explode. The sweat ran down into my eyes and my mouth, blurring and stinging. All the while, I dug my fingers deeper into Resi's hand. She kept pace until we reached the edge of the woods where crouched figures darted back and forth. Before I could stop, a hand reached out, dragged me to the ground, and held me down. Resi sobbed uncontrollably next to me.

"Damn you! Are you possessed by the devil, running in the line of fire like that?" The angry German soldier snapped, "Stay down now and don't you move until I tell you to."

The soldier left momentarily. The staccato burst of machine guns shredded the outlying areas of the forest, and our soldiers returned the fire. Resi and I covered our ears and lay still until the hellish noise around us abated. We looked up and we saw our soldiers crawling, running, and pausing behind trees. Suddenly they were out of sight.

"Resi," I cried out, "we better run!" Wordlessly, she followed me along the walk path. We crouched in ditches, ran and walked, until we saw the outskirts of our town in the distance. The group of soldiers we had seen in the woods had broken ranks and they now moved sporadically away from the front line.

Once in a while, they would yell, "Get away from here before the enemy gets you."

An older soldier stopped us. "Here," he said, "take this and hold it up high when you see the enemy soldiers."

He handed me a white piece of cloth and walked on.

"Thank you, Mister," I said. He waved as he left.

Resi asked, "The Americans or Russians won't shoot us if we give up first, will they?"

"I have no idea what they will do when we hold up the piece of cloth. Just don't eat anything the soldiers give you. Remember, we were warned on the radio not to eat anything because the Americans poison what they give us. Watch out especially for chocolate and chewing gum."

"Anneliese, what is this chewing gum?" Resi wondered.

"I am sure we will find out. Just refuse it, whatever it is. I wish Mama were here," I sighed, "She should have known better, she should have stayed home."

We had reached the city limits, and the eerie stillness frightened me. Homes along the street were shut down, shutters were closed to protect the windows, and doors were bolted. I saw no one on the street as we approached the market square. The tree near the church bore no evidence of the violence it held the night before. The dead soldier was no longer hanging, and the church yard was void of wounded soldiers. Yet, I felt the dead soldier's presence, and the cries of the wounded soldiers' jerked my memory.

I moved closer to Resi and sought comfort in her nearness. "Ten more minutes and we will be home," I reassured her.

"Maybe we should go to Uncle Pepp," she pleaded.

"No, we are going home. I told Mama so."

Finally, we rounded the curve. "Resi, there is the house. It is still standing. Isn't it beautiful?" I cried out and broke into a run. "Come on! Run! Run!"

I squeezed her hand, and shouted, "We are alive . . . and we are home!" Tears ran down my cheeks and they momentarily blocked my view.

White makeshift flags fluttered at the windows of every house on our street, though not a person was in sight. I fastened the white cloth the soldier had given me onto the gate's hinges and I raced toward the house.

"I'll get the keys from the wood pile," Resi called. The keys jangled as she threw them toward me. "Hurry, Anneliese, open up!"

Once inside, I locked the door and checked throughout the house. Everything was in order. The horrors of yesterday had not reached our home. Resi broke the silence. "I'm hungry, what can we eat?"

I rummaged through the cupboard. "I don't see any food, Mama must have taken everything with her. Maybe later we can try and milk the goat, but for now we wait and keep the doors locked. I guess looking out the window won't hurt." Terrified, I stepped back and called out, "Resi, come look! American tanks are coming down the street. What are we going to do?"

Scarcely breathing, we watched the huge, camouflaged tanks clamoring by. Their creaky tracks hid the surface of the narrow road while their big guns bobbed up and down. Invisible drivers maneuvered the monstrous machines without hesitation, while a few foot soldiers with guns drawn, walked cautiously alongside. Now, the whole city was draped in white cloth, but the streets were still vacant. Everyone was cautiously waiting.

The uncertainty of what lay ahead kept Resi and me silent. I kept my fears about Mama's, Max's, and Irmgard's fate to myself. I wondered when, and if, we would see them again.

Americans coming to our town.

CHAPTER TWENTY-TWO

WAR'S AFTERMATH

I longed for Mama. Guilt-ridden, I opened the window and watched with apprehension as several American soldiers and a group of civilians walked by.

"Resi, I think the forced labor workers are coming, just like Mama said." We crouched down and watched for a moment, but I couldn't stand the mounting tension any longer. I whispered, "Let's hide, quickly."

Before we could figure out where to hide, someone called, "Peppi, open up! Open up! It is all right!"

I pushed the curtains apart. "Let them in!" I urged. "It is Wiedold , Kasha, and Roman...Uncle Pepp's foreign-labor workers."

"I am so glad you are here!" I called out. "Roman, is the war over?"

"For us, yes, our days of working for your Uncle Pepp as foreign labor workers are over," Roman said, "but what the future holds for you, I don't know. Lucky for you that Pepp treated us well, so now we will help him. He asked us in his best manners if we would stay with Peppi, while homes get looted."

"Roman, be quiet." Wiedold turned toward me. "We will stay here until the looting is over."

When rowdiness erupted near the front entrance, Wiedold and Roman opened the window and spoke Polish to the men and women below. They shouted, shook their fists, and pointed at the houses on the street as they left.

"Where is Peppi and where are the little ones?" Kasha asked.

"They are in Dobrigau, in a barn," I answered.

"Peppi ran and left you here? Not Peppi!"

Resi extended her index finger toward me and piped up, "She ran away, she left Mama there, and now, we are here alone."

"Anneliese, how could you?" Kasha scolded. "Just wait until your Uncle hears that! He won't like it at all."

"It is decided," Wiedold interrupted, "I will take you to Pepp."

"But I have to stay here," I argued, "Mama thinks I am at home."

"You will go to Pepp. I am not going to be responsible for your welfare, and Resi, you must come too."

Wiedold took us on the street and he walked between us with his arm around my shoulder. "Anneliese," he warned, "let me do the talking and don't ask questions or argue. It is extremely dangerous out here."

Wiedold didn't need to worry; my mouth was dry, I had lost my voice, and I was scared of the groups of foreign workers who walked in and out of homes while others danced euphorically in the streets. We saw men and women who carried radios, clothes, clocks, and other household items they had looted. We ducked because what they didn't want came flying through the window panes. Several workers pointed at Resi and me, Wiedold shouted back in Polish, and their wanton gestures and laughter made me shiver.

A huge, white flag hung from the church steeple, American military vehicles drove through the streets, and I caught a glimpse of American foot soldiers entering German homes. Resi and I clung to Wiedold until we finally entered the bakery. Several American soldiers looked up at Aunt Nannie, Uncle Pepp, Erna, Joey, and Grandma as they came down the stairs with their hands held high. Aunt Nannie, barely five feet tall, and blocking the width of the curved stairs with her corpulent body, shouted, "I'll give up! I'll give up!" Then she turned toward Uncle Pepp. "Pepp, get your hands up," she ordered and without taking her eyes off the soldiers, she blocked Uncle Pepp and would not let him pass.

One of the soldiers advanced to the stairs and motioned for Aunt Nannie to step down. With lightning speed they body searched everyone, and then motioned to Uncle Pepp and commanded, "Come. Come."

We watched as they searched the bakery, the farm equipment

shed and the storage rooms, while we were confined to the kitchen. Wiedold told Aunt Nannie why we were here, and she shook her head.

"Pepp won't like what you did Anneliese. You just don't leave your mother like that."

Just then, the soldiers and a transformed Uncle Pepp returned. He was smiling broadly as he smoked his first American cigarette and, to the delight of the American soldiers, he ceremoniously blew patterns of smoke rings into the air. Erna and Aunt Nannie served the men slices of bread and glasses of black market wine. The soldiers toasted and nodded their approval. They talked, they came toward us and offered us a cigarette.

Uncle Pepp spurred us on. "As of now, everyone here smokes, so you just better take that cigarette. You hear me? Everyone! Smoke!"

Erna, Joey, Resi, and I joined the smokers. The soldiers were amused as we choked and coughed, while Grandma looked sternly at Uncle Pepp. When Aunt Nannie offered more wine, the soldiers declined and left.

Instantly, Uncle Pepp commanded, "Put your cigarettes out now! You will smoke only when the Americans offer you a cigarette. Don't inhale, just fake it. Now, you will give your cigarettes to me."

Wiedold explained Mama's absence, and Uncle Pepp, concerned with other matters, decided, "You and Resi will stay here. Erna, they will sleep with you, your bed is big enough."

We felt safe in Uncle Pepp's home, but we were glad when Wiedold fetched us during the afternoon. "Anneliese," he said, "you won't find your home as clean and tidy as you left it, but after five years at forced labor, we finally had the victory party we always dreamt about. A relief agency brought us drinks and food we hadn't seen in years."

"Are you going back to Poland now that you have won the war?" I asked.

"I didn't win a thing. I lost everything. My family and my home are gone. The Russians are occupying our village, and I have heard that the Russians accuse us of collaborating with the Germans. What a joke! No, I will not return. I will stay here and keep baking for Pepp until I can see more clearly what the future holds for me."

As we approached our house with Wiedold, the front door was wide open. Mama, Max and Irmgard had just returned from Dobrigau.

"You are safe!" Mama folded her hands. "Thank you, God, you kept them from harm."

"Mama got sick this morning, and it is your fault, all your fault," Max shouted at me.

Mama came toward me and I was startled by the intense anger I saw in her eyes. She grabbed my shoulders and fiercely shook me as she asked, "How could you put me through such agony during the past twenty-four hours? I was almost out of my mind. What if something had happened to you, or to us? What would you have done?" Tears streamed down her cheeks and sobs shook her body as she turned from me and cried.

"Mama," I pleaded, "I had to get home. I just couldn't stand living in that filthy barn. We would have been better off at home."

"Who could know what is right or wrong during times like these. I thought I did what was best for us." Mama relented.

We ate the scraps of food Wiedold and his friends had left for us, and we cleaned until exhaustion overtook us. Now that we didn't fear for our safety or our lives we looked forward to a good night's sleep. We thanked God that the Americans had taken our town instead of the Russians, and we hoped we could look toward better days. But things got worse. We were jolted awake during the early morning hours by loud voices outside, and the din of war vehicles. Mama looked out the window and cried out, "It's the Americans! They are in our garden."

Still in her nightgown, she ran and opened the door. Alongside an American officer stood an interpreter, "Ma'am, you and the children will have to leave, so take blankets, clothing, money, ration cards, ID's, several cooking utensils and towels. You will be housed in the former Hitler Youth building down the street, and the soldiers will move in here."

Mama asked, " How long will we have to stay there?"

"I don't know. Just get moving. After you leave, you will not be allowed to come back while the soldiers occupy your home. You have thirty minutes to get your things together," the interpreter said.

We were stunned. Mama directed, "Wear several layers of

clothing, fill your pockets with smaller items, and each one of you will carry as much as you can down to the hand wagon. I hope they will let us take the radio, we need to hear what is going on."

The soldiers waited in the foyer and in the garden as we walked by. I barely looked at them as we passed. Just then, a soldier stepped in front of Mama, took the radio from her, and without a word, put it in his Army truck.

"Mama," Max cried out, "he can't take our radio. He is stealing it, isn't he?"

"Never mind, Max. Just push the wagon. Hurry, let's get to the Hitler Youth Home," Mama urged.

All along the street, neighbors were dislodged from their homes. Grandpas and grandmas led or carried their frightened grandchildren. Older siblings carried their own bedding and their mamas went back and forth gathering cooking utensils and clothing. Buchka's German shepherd strained on his chain. He moved constantly back and forth while he barked and bared his sharp teeth. We entered the Hitler Youth Home where neighbors, who had moved in already, opened the straw bundles that had been left behind by the KLV, and they spread loose straw on the floor. Grandpa Schiller, being the elder, took charge. "I counted," he said. "We will need at least sixty spaces. Compared to other dislodged families, we are well off because we have a small kitchen, tables, and long benches. There are several bathrooms, but as far as washing is concerned we will talk about it later. Each family will bed in its assigned area, and everyone must keep their space neat and clean. I don't know how long we will be here, but if we want order, we have to enforce rules and regulations while we are together."

"How will we get our food and our rations?" Anni asked.

"I heard we are under curfew," Miss Hoff told us. "We may go out in the morning from ten to noon and during the afternoon from two to four, but that's it. The Americans have set up various check points where you must show your ID. I will translate during emergencies."

During the next few hours, families formed groups almost identical to the neighborhoods they lived in. Mothers huddled together anxiously and wondered about tomorrow's food rations and other needed items. As night fell, lights were limited to the big hall and ten o'clock was bedtime for everyone. During the nocturnal hours, babies cried, small children had bad dreams, and the snoring or coughing sounds of the elders awoke the soundest sleeper. Morning hours fell into routines. The sick and the children had first claim on the available water, then everyone else took turns. Grandpas and grandmas took over and intervened when the little ones could not settle their little quarrels. Grandpa Schiller settled the arguments of the adults, and he always got his way when he advised, "If you don't like it here, maybe you can join the refugees. One of them will gladly take your space."

Curfew was exactly like Miss Hoff had told us. It was so hard to walk by during open hours and watch the soldiers moving in and out of our homes. We realized that their lives were different from ours; there was no shortage of wine and liquor, food and fresh fruit were brought in by the truckloads. On nice days, we could hear their music blaring as soon as we stepped out of the Hitler Youth Home, and we saw girls come and go. The soldiers tried to start conversations when Anni, Resi, and I walked by.

"Hey, Blondie, you speak English?"

We shook our heads.

"Come! come."

"No. No," we answered and walked past.

Since our rations remained the same as during the last weeks of the war, we still were always hungry. We took to the fields or ditches instead of the roads because, frequently, the soldiers threw out candy bars or slices of bread. Clutching the handouts we had caught, we ran alongside the vehicles and yelled "Thank you, thank you," while the soldiers laughed.

When we learned that the soldiers would occupy our homes for additional weeks, we resigned ourselves to communal living. Mama and Anni avoided the trouble makers, watched our belongings, and we always kept our food rations within sight until we ate them. Grandpa Schiller, a World War I cavalry corporal, kept a tight control over his domain, his family of sixty individuals.

CHAPTER TWENTY-THREE

REVELATIONS

It was a Monday morning; the weather was dreary, it drizzled, and the cold north wind kept everyone inside. Max and Irmgard were playing while Resi and I sat on a bench near Mama.

Anni and Mama were talking softly, "Peppi, you can't go on like this. How far along are you?"

Mama pleaded, "Anni, just drop it."

"Peppi, you can't hide it any longer," Anni urged. "How far along are you?"

"Mama, what is she talking about?" I interrupted.

Anni turned toward me, "Anneliese, you don't know? Your Mama is pregnant. Can't you see that?"

"Mama! You can't be?"

Mama's eyes filled with tears, she nodded and whispered, "Yes, Anneliese, I am pregnant."

"But, but, Mama ... ?"

"Let me be right now. I will talk with you later."

"Anni," Mama sighed, "now you know for sure, I am pregnant. I thought your Papa would be home before I had to face all this."

We became aware that everyone looked at Mama and it was dead-still in the room. Resi stared straight ahead, not looking at anyone, while I left the room and sat down on the cold entrance steps. Why didn't I know? Although Mama had been on edge and worried, all this time I had thought it was the daily struggle for survival. But now I knew the truth. Momentarily, Resi came out and sat down beside me.

"Resi, did you know?"

"No, how would I know? I am younger than you."

Mama joined us. She reached for my hand and pleaded, "Anneliese, I was with Papa the end of November. But this is not the time to talk, since nothing will change immediately. We can wait until we get back into our home."

I had so many questions I wanted to ask, but the way Mama looked at me, defeated, pleading, her body shaking violently . . . I just couldn't go on.

"It is nearly ten o'clock. We will need our milk and bread rations, so you will go this morning," she said, holding on to me, exhausted and strained. "Anneliese, right now you think so much has changed, but you will see we can survive if we work together as a family."

Days ran into weeks. I felt better being in the Hitler Youth Home because Mama's friends and I shared our concern about her well-being. She was so exhausted and I had never seen her so depressed.

Frequently, Mama lamented, "Why now? How can I bring another little one into chaos and times of starvation?"

"Peppi, we made it through the war, so a little baby isn't going to scare us; we will get through this, too," Anni consoled. "We will help out where we can and Max should come home from Berlin soon."

A month had passed by when we finally were told that the American soldiers were transferred and we could move back into our homes. We expected the worst as we returned.

Max ran for the shed. "I hope they fed the rabbits." He came back, crying out, "They didn't. The rabbits and chickens are gone, all gone, and the goats are skinny."

Mama held him, while he wept and shouted angrily, "Why did the Americans kill our animals? Now we have no meat and the goats may die, too."

"Max, I will talk with Pepp, he will see what he can do. Thank God that someone fed the goats. We just have to manage."

The disorder we found was a nightmare, but we took consolation in the fact that our "guests" had left the dirty dishes intact while several of our neighbors found that their dishes, pots and utensils had been thrown through windows until the cupboards were bare. We even found food, and the presence of food made the hours and days of cleaning pass smoothly.

Throughout all the turmoil, Mama's pregnancy was on our minds. One evening after Irmgard and Max were asleep, Mama said, "Resi, Anneliese, I know my pregnancy is something no one wanted, but, I am pregnant."

I was relieved when Resi asked, "What does Papa say?" Mama sighed. "I don't think he knows that I am pregnant since the mail service to the ever-changing front has been non-existent for quite some time. But I pray that Papa will come home soon, and times will get better."

We hoped, but day by day our living conditions worsened. The outskirts of the town teemed with refugees. Since every home was filled to capacity, refugees lived outdoors in makeshift tents, they bathed in the nearby brook and relieved themselves in the surrounding bushes. Children followed the American soldiers and begged for chocolate, while homeless KLV teenagers traded their young bodies for food and shelter. Hunger-driven hordes perched themselves on the edges of the American field kitchens and waited for the food refuse that was dumped daily.

Mama watched us closely and she told us, "I always want to know where you are, who you are with and what you're doing. You must keep to the curfew, don't get into trouble, and stay away from the American soldiers."

Mama had good reasons to show concern. After Uncle Pepp brought two rabbits and chickens, Max was eager to get acquainted with the American soldiers. Their big trucks, guns, and easy-going manner drew Max to the soldiers who guarded the German Prisoners of War across the street from us. He came home with his pockets filled with chocolate or crackers.

"I could get more," he said. "I told the American soldiers that I had two blonde sisters. I bet you could get chocolate, too. I can speak American." He pointed at his eyes, "Augen ... eyes, Nase ... nose, Mund ... mouth. I learn new words everyday. You should come, I bet you'll learn to speak American. It is so easy! Anneliese, where is Texas? The soldiers always sing about Texas."

Mama was torn. "I let Max go to the Americans because we do hear some news about our soldiers in the camp," she said. "Max is still a child and he thinks everyone is his friend. We must help him while he learns about the real world."

Day and night our soldiers, flanked by their captors, arrived on foot or on American army trucks. We watched as the Americans took the wounded prisoners to the hospitals in Waldsassen while the captured SS men were transferred to various destinations. Anxiously, we stood in line and waited for the posting of new POW names at the market square and we walked away quietly because Papa was not listed.

Finally, we were allowed to come near the camp where we called out the names of our loved ones and cheered for the fortunate family members who heard some news about their sons or fathers. We saw that the American transports could not cope with the influx of new POWS, so sometimes the prisoners' rations were much less than ours. Anni, Resi, and I collected scraps of food and cupfuls of water from anyone who was willing to share. The boys collected wood scraps and built a fire outside. We cooked what we had collected in an old kettle and we dragged and carried the hot mush to the Prisoner of War camp.

As we neared the gate, an American soldier spoke to the guards, and then he came toward Anni and me. I briefly felt his hand on mine as he motioned that he wanted the kettle.

"No," I said, but Anni suggested, "Just set the kettle on the gravel path, and see what he does."

The soldier motioned to us, "Come," he picked the kettle up and carried it into the camp. Our soldiers rushed forward, but the American held them back until our men formed a line and waited their turn. The line was too long for the food we had, but we ladled the mush onto each soldier's tin dish while they thanked us. "This is the first food we had in two days. The American soldiers tell us their food transport will come tomorrow."

All this time, the American had stood aside and watched. He was tall, and slim. His light-brown hair was parted on the left side and combed straight across his high forehead. As we ran out of food, he came over and asked, "OK?" His big blue eyes held my gaze and he broke into a smile, "OK?" he asked again. We thanked him, "Danke, danke," but he just shook his head, returned to his jeep, and drove off.

"Now *there* is a gentleman," Anni said as we walked away.

Within a few days the American food transports arrived regularly, and curfew hours were extended. The long summer days and relatively few restrictions for the soldiers were the reasons why Mama cautioned us, "The Americans are men on the loose. They won the war and they are out to have a good time while they are here. As I said before, stay away from them."

We obeyed Mama, but Max didn't. His pockets were bursting at the seams with candies, chocolate, and chewing gum, as he declared, "I told some nice American officers where we live. I think they are coming to see you."

Before we could answer, a jeep stopped by the garden gate. Two officers sat in back, and one called out in fluent German, "Hey, Fraulein, we are coming tonight about eight, we'll bring food and drink, and we will have a party."

"No, no," we begged off.

They laughed, "Relax, we'll see you then."

Mama scolded Max, "What have you done? I don't want any problems."

"I know that nice American who helped me with the mush comes to the POW camp every day," I told Mama. "I will ask him to take these officers somewhere else."

"How will you do that? You know the officers can enter our home whenever they want. Does that soldier speak German, too?"

I found a way. Resi and I used the German-English dictionary, and we labored over the translation of our request. "Please take your officers away, NOT OUR HOUSE! Thank you."

Finally, late that afternoon, the gentleman-soldier's jeep stopped at the POW camp. I took Resi's hand. "Come on, let's give him the note!"

Startled, the soldier caught the note I thrust at him. "Party?" he asked.

I shook my head, "No, no. Nix Ok?"

He looked puzzled. "Officers?" he asked.

"See, he can't do anything," Resi retorted.

"Oh, yes, he can." I replied.

I looked imploringly at the American and begged, "You come my house?"

He nodded and smiled, "Yes, yes!" He drew the number eight

on the paper and said, "Eight o'clock."

Resi stood there with her mouth wide open. She sputtered, "But, but, . . . Anneliese, that wasn't in the plan. He should take the officers somewhere else, but now he is coming to our house, too. What will Mama say?"

"We are not going to tell her. Why worry her?"

Shortly before eight our gentleman-soldier, as we called him, came. He hurriedly entered the hallway, looked around and said, "Here," as he disappeared behind Mama's bedroom door.

Before Mama could ask for an explanation, the boisterous voices of four Americans who greeted us cheerily demanded our attention.

"They came to see you," Max explained while he hugged his bulging pockets. He pointed at us, "Anneliese and Resi, blond, just like I said."

"Mama, you got a nice boy here, very bright," one of the officers said in fluent German.

"No, not bright at all," Mama said.

Soon cigarette smoke clouded the room. The Americans toasted, "To peace, to girls, and to Mama before she goes to bed."

"No! I won't go to bed, ever," Mama said. "I stay up with my girls until you leave."

The officers finally gave in. "Mama, you are OK. We'll finish our drinks, then we leave and find a real party, OK?" With that, they left.

The American soldier inquired through the partially opened door, "Gone?"

I nodded. He came into the hallway, "Good," he said.

Mama and Resi returned to the kitchen. I just stood there. I liked the soldier's smile, his sparkling blue eyes, and his mannerism. He pointed at himself, 'Kenny.'" He nodded, "You?"

"Anneliese," I said.

"Anneliese," he repeated.

His smile and his eyes sparkled even more, I thought. I felt drawn to him.

I stepped closer. "Thank you."

Mama opened the kitchen door just then. "Is he still here?"

"He is leaving."

The soldier understood. "Auf Wiedersehen," he said and walked out.

The next night he stopped by. "You, Mama, Ok?" he asked.

"Yes," I assured him.

He pointed at his comrade and said, "Ruther."

Mama looked uneasy as we walked into the kitchen.

"What now?" she asked.

"Mama, he wanted to know if we were all right. I couldn't just stay outside with them, and he, after all, was concerned about us."

Our conversing was easier since Ruther spoke some German and with the German-English dictionary by our side, we discovered that we could play checkers and rummy until it was time for them to leave.

CHAPTER TWENTY-FOUR

THE GENTLEMAN-SOLDIER

After that visit, Kenny came back almost nightly. Within a week, he had captivated the whole family with his easy-going, respectful manner. He often held little Irmgard, and he was truly concerned about the impetigo that covered her skinny body. One evening he came with a box under his arm. He put the box down, he picked Irmgard up, and he said, "All go, Mama stay," and he motioned again for us to leave. Resi, Max and I wondered why we had to leave.

Resi asked, "What did he have in that box?"

"What is he doing? Max pondered. "He isn't a doctor. He doesn't even look like one to me."

Almost an hour had past before Mama called us, "Come in, and look at Irmgard." White gauze covered her every inch of skin. All we could see were her big, blue eyes, and her lips.

Max looked at her and exclaimed, "Mama, now we have a mummy in our house. How long will she be like that?"

Mama wiped away tears, and said, "For three days. I think Kenny will come back and watch over Irmgard."

Four days later, Mama and Kenny repeated the process again, and Irmgard, unlike other infected children, started healing without infections. Kenny's concern also shifted toward Mama's well-being. He helped Resi and me with household chores, and impressed Anni and her family with his polite mannerism. Almost nightly, he walked the five miles from Waldsassen to Mitterteich and then back to Waldsassen. By now it was apparent to everyone that he walked this distance so he could be with me.

I knew I liked Kenny — more than I should, but then I had so many reasons to like him.   He liked everyone in the family, and he made us laugh when we tried to converse.   When I wondered if America had Lemon Butterflies, Kenny assured me that many people in America loved their canaries.

He listened closely as I talked and pantomimed how Max and I searched the woods for dead branches and trees, felled and piled them on the wagon, and pushed and pulled until we made it safely home. He shook his head at the blisters on my hands and the tar and cuts on my feet. One day, he pulled me toward him, and in front of Mama, he kissed my sore hands and scraped the tar from my feet. I knew then that I loved him because he was nicer than any man I knew.

That night, Mama said, "Anneliese, we must talk."

"Mama, I know what you will say. It's about Kenny, isn't it?"

"Yes. I see how you look at him. Remember what you were taught. You must treat your body with respect because your body and your good name are the best things you will ever have. Protect both."

"Mama ...," I interrupted, but she continued.

"Men like to forget that a woman should stay a virgin until she marries. As Uncle Pepp so crudely says, 'It is the woman who needs to let the man know how far he can go. All she has to do is say 'no' and keep her legs together.'"

I covered my ears. I felt uneasy, hearing talk like that. "Mama," I pleaded, "you don't have to say any more. I know all that."

She removed my hands. "I can't say it often enough. I want to save you a lot of grief, so you listen and do as I say. Anneliese, if Kenny truly loves you, let him prove it. Make him understand you will do the right thing and you will wait until you are married . . . When a man marries you, he commits himself, and he is then responsible for your well-being, he has to support you and the children you will bear. Can you remember Marie Schliesser? She became pregnant without marriage.   Rudie went on his way unscathed while Marie was left with a child and her ruined reputation. Anneliese, I trust you, and I expect you will not shame us. You know that eventually Kenny has to return to America and he, and you will learn to go on with your lives. So promise me, you will not give in to Kenny's or your desires. After that, I will say no more."

Mama looked solemnly at me and waited.

"I promise, Mama."

"You promise what?"

"I promise I will wait until I am married. That promise should be easy for me to keep since so far, you know that we have never been alone."

"Believe me, Anneliese, I have my reasons. What I ask of you is for your own good and the family reputation which, right now, is at a low point, anyhow."

Mama had talked with me just in time because my feelings for Kenny had grown into love. Since I had met him, the evenings began for me when I spied him in his Army uniform with his rifle at his side. Even after the long, five mile walk from Waldsassen, he always waved and smiled as he approached our garden gate. He greeted everyone and then I knew that Mama trusted me when she took Irmgard, Max and Resi to the garden, or for walks, so that Kenny and I could have some time alone. We hugged and kissed and embraced until I wished that my body could be one with his. No man had ever held me so tightly, yet tenderly. At night after he set out on his walk, I dreamt of him, longed to be his, and wished we were husband and wife.

"Anneliese, come to America, to Minnesota," Kenny said one evening.

"Minnesota?" I asked, while my heart pounded wildly.

"Yes. Crookston, Minnesota, nice, but winter cold." Kenny hugged himself and shivered.

"Here, winter cold." I shivered much longer than he.

"No, no," he laughed. "Minnesota ice, snow, cold wind. Six months."

He came close to me and repeated, "Yes, you come to Minnesota. You my wife? Yes?"

I threw my arms around him, "Yes! Yes!" I cried out, "I come Minnesota."

My happiness knew no bounds. Because Mama had thought that Kenny would never marry me, and since I could only imagine how she would react, I kept Kenny's proposal a secret. We located Minnesota on our globe and with our German-English dictionary at hand, we found joy as we discovered new, common words while the similarities and differences of our people and countries drew us closer together. We, who had been through the horrors of war, envisioned that we had a future. Life, hope, and love were beckoning us and secretly, eagerly, I hoped for a future with Kenny.

Kenny

CHAPTER TWENTY-FIVE

NO MORE SECRETS

So far, Kenny's circle of acquaintances consisted of my immediate family, Anni's family, and Frau Rahn, the midwife. I hoped Uncle Pepp would never hear about Kenny and how much he meant to me. Aunt Anna, Uncle Franz's wife, changed all that on a beautiful Sunday afternoon: Kenny had just arrived when Irmgard looked out the window and remarked, "There is Aunt Anna. I think she is coming here."

Mama joined Irmgard. "Yes, she is."

"Mama, what are we going to do with Kenny?" I asked.

"Take him out of here, right now," she said.

I pulled Kenny's arm, "Come!" I led him into Mama's bedroom.

He looked startled. "What?" he mumbled.

"Here," I motioned to the chair. "You stay, OK? I come here."

He reached for me and tried to take me in his arms. "No, I must go." His kiss brushed my cheek before I closed the door.

Mama was still at the window, watching Aunt Anna's approach. I rushed toward Irmgard. "Baby sister," I said, "you and I have a secret. Don't you tell Aunt Anna about Kenny; don't tell her he is here. Be nice and quiet while she is visiting and Kenny will bring you a treat."

Irmgard smiled. "I will never tell."

Aunt Anna entered and we knew we were in for a lengthy visit when she propped the sofa pillows up behind her back and made herself comfortable. She always knew the most recent gossip and everything else that was going on in town. Aunt Anna never kept us in suspense. She immediately started in.

"Peppi, I think it is a disgrace how some of our women and girls throw themselves at the American soldiers. Why, it is disgusting. These men just want more than a friendly ..." She paused while she looked at Irmgard, and then back to Mama and me. "You know what I mean. These men don't care how old our women and girls are, they don't care whether they are married or not, they just sleep with them and have their fun. Then they go home and brag about the swell times they had with our women . . . all for a chocolate bar. Hm!"

Irmgard was fidgeting and getting restless. I looked at her; I motioned for her to be quiet.

Aunt Anna was in her element. "You know about the two refugee girls who went off with two American soldiers ... well, the soldiers are back, but the girls never came home. Tell me, where are they?"

"Who knows what the girls decided to do," Mama interrupted. "They may have found a better camp."

"Oh, Peppi, how can you stick up for them? Why, right in your neighborhood, Lotti Hammers got shot at by one of their drunken soldiers. I hear you and other neighbors saw it. So you should know: Those American soldiers are no good."

Suddenly, Irmgard stood up. "That's not true! The soldiers are nice."

Aunt Anna looked stunned. Momentarily, she was struck speechless, then she mocked, "Why, you little know-it-all! When did you get so smart? You don't even know any soldiers."

Irmgard met Aunt Anna's challenge head-on. Before we could intervene, she blurted out, "I do too know soldiers. I know Kenny. I am his Second Lady and he fixed my impetigo. He brings me treats and he is just like us."

"Just where is this Kenny you know?" Aunt Anna baited.

Irmgard looked frightened, but stood her ground. "He is right here, in Mama's bedroom," she blurted out. Tears streamed down her cheeks as she cried out, "Now you made me tell and I promised Anneliese I would keep our secret!"

Aunt Anna's eyes glistened. Her face was flushed as she took a deep breath. "Peppi," she retorted, "you mean you have an

American soldier right here hiding in your own bedroom? No wonder you stick up for them. Such goings-on in your home! Poor Max, just wait 'till he comes home."

She moved toward the kitchen door, but Mama blocked her exit. "Anna, you will have to wait. For the good of everyone, you will not meet our soldier today."

Aunt Anna sat down, again. "Peppi, what will Max say when he comes home and finds an enemy soldier hidden in his bedroom? In bright daylight, yet! Have you no shame, no concern ? What about the Solch family reputation? What will people say?" Aunt Anna questioned.

"Anna, if you leave it alone, people won't know." Mama answered. "But we will handle it. For now, there is nothing more to say."

Aunt Anna stood up. "This is terrible. You don't know where Max is; I don't know where Franz and Hans are; and my poor Lisl, she is in the East where the Russians rape women and even twelve-year-old girls. Here, the American soldiers take our girls. Peppi, you just better take care of your girls. Don't allow them to be alone with that soldier. I just know it, he is up to no good!" She stopped her avalanche of reprimands and sighed. "Well, I must get home now."

Stunned into silence, we watched as Aunt Anna took to the road with walk-run motions. "Anneliese, now everyone will know you are seeing an American soldier," Mama remarked. "Pepp will be furious and Grandma surely will have something to say. Now you will have to face the consequences and it will not be easy." She took Irmgard from Resi and she stroked her hair. "Don't you blame Irmgard, either. She feels bad enough. I knew this couldn't go on, because nothing remains a secret forever. In a way, I am glad it is out in the open. How you handle the talk in town and all the questions will be your decision. Now fetch Kenny."

I returned to Mama's bedroom, and through the partially opened French window I faced an empty yard. I raced outside and with his arms wide open, Kenny came toward me and asked, "Anneliese, OK?"

"Aunt Anna, no good," I muttered.

Kenny pointed at his watch. "I late, must go now. See you tomorrow."

The next morning on the way to the bakery, I felt people were staring at me and I quickened my steps until I reached the bakery.

Erna met me. "Anneliese, is Papa ever angry! Go into his office before someone tells him you are here."

The scowl on Uncle Pepp's face deepened. "Just tell me, is it true that you fraternize with an American soldier and yet, you hide him when people come? What kind of clandestine affair is that? I always knew you were impetuous and strong willed, but what has gotten into your mother? I can't understand why she didn't stop such an unthinkable relationship." Uncle Pepp thundered, "Well, it is not too late to stop it now, and stop it will."

"Uncle Pepp, Kenny is always a gentleman, so why should I stop seeing him?"

"Because there is not one Bavarian man who will touch you after you have been involved with an American soldier."

"I don't want a Bavarian man."

"Don't you get off the subject. I must talk with your mama and that will be the end of your infatuation. You always go against rules. Why, if you were my daughter that would never have happened because I just would forbid it and that would end it."

There was a knock, Grandma entered, and she turned toward me. "You are just like your papa. He always did what he wanted and you are just the same. Pepp, don't wait, talk with Peppi. Anneliese, you must talk with Father Neidl. Maybe he can bring you to your senses."

"No! I won't! I haven't done anything wrong. Why should I go and see Father Neidl? Anyway, I must go home. Mama isn't feeling well, it's the baby."

"I do think you should take responsibility for your mama's not feeling well. I had eleven babies, they don't make a woman sick when she is that far along, they just come. So don't you blame a little baby for the problems you cause. Go home. We will take care of this intolerable situation."

Like a thief, I took the back roads home. When I arrived, Mama took me in her arms, and looked at me with pain in her eyes. "Anneliese, you are making life so hard for yourself, and after today, it will get even harder. You will have to choose. Kenny is a wonderful man, caring, responsible and trustworthy, but he is not from here. Our countries are not at peace. You two won't be able to marry, so where will your relationship lead?"

"Mama, Kenny will go home and then he will come back."

Suddenly, Mama held her stomach. The baby was kicking, and she was breathing in intervals as she said, "I must lie down for a while so you must take care of things here."

Left by myself, I was scared and longed for the past when I believed the stork brought babies. How simple it was then. We walked to the storks' nest and called out,

> "Stork, stork, you are good.
> Please bring me a brother."

> "Stork, stork, you are the best.
> Please, bring me a sister."

I was way into my adolescence and I, like many others, sang along when the stork song was played on the radio,

> "On the roof of the world, there stands a stork nest
> with a hundred-thousand little babies in it.

> "If you like one, and you'll marry me, the stork will bring such a little baby to you. You needn't be scared, it doesn't hurt at all. The stork will bite you in the left leg, and then ... everything is great!"

> "On the roof of the world, there stands a stork nest, with a hundred-thousand little babies in it."

Life was so hard now. Kenny and I had no control; no one cared what we wanted. I fumed. I was sick of all the talk and reprimands. Come to my senses? I was 18 going on 19...too young for Kenny and too old for puppy love? Why couldn't the adults leave me alone? I didn't do anything wrong.

My anger rose. I was glad that they didn't know he had asked me to come to America. I'd show them! Memories of motion pictures and stories of America filled my mind. Determination gripped me: I will go to that wonderful land and Kenny and I will be happy forever. That night, I found that once again Mama had been right. It was good that Kenny's visits were no longer a 'clandestine affair' because Uncle Pepp stopped by.

"I will check that American out for myself," he said.

Kenny, oblivious of the family conflict, smiled at Uncle Pepp and offered him a cigarette. Uncle Pepp inhaled deeply. "Fine cigarettes," he said.

Kenny offered the package. "Yes, yes."

Uncle Pepp looked at me while he took several cigarettes.

"Kenny doesn't speak German," I said.

Uncle Pepp's eyes widened, "How do you communicate?"

I pushed the dictionary toward him. "With the dictionary. It takes time, but believe me, it works."

"He seems like a nice enough man, but I tell you this war made some of us a little crazy." He looked toward Kenny. "He doesn't even speak German." Pushing the dictionary away, Uncle Pepp continued. "I am not going to talk to a man with a dictionary in my hand. I never have and I never will. Anneliese, you just better mind your manners and behave until the Americans leave. Then you can be normal again." He turned toward Mama. "Peppi, now you can see what Max and you get for bringing your daughters up to be independent. In my book they need a father to tell them what to do until they are married. Then the husband can take over and keep them in line." Uncle Pepp rose, shook hands with Kenny, and left.

I dreaded going into town for our rations, since I knew people in town were talking about me. My former classmates stopped talking when I joined them, and their mothers who used to smile and chat with me, humiliated me now. They showed their disapproval by walking to the other side of the street, or they looked away and ignored my greeting. When I stood in line for food, someone would fake surprise and ask, "Don't the American men supply what their girls need?"

"Why should they, when a chocolate bar does the trick?" someone said. I complained to Anni, "I wish those busybodies could find something else to talk about."

CHAPTER TWENTY-SIX

MAN'S INHUMANITY TO MAN — LIFE GOES ON

Within days, people in town did have something new to talk about. The town's grapevine of the back roads and Main Street was exploding with stories of atrocities committed by our SS troops. We learned that millions of Jews had been incarcerated in concentration camps near and far. We didn't want to believe the pictures of camps equipped with gas showers and ovens. We couldn't look at the deep graves that hid hundreds to thousands of nameless, skeletal humans without feeling shame and guilt. We asked ourselves, "How could six million Jews die? How could we not know? How could we not even suspect?"

I remembered the final days of the war. I remembered the concentration camp prisoners as they left their column, and came into our yard desperate for food and water. I still could hear the voices of the guards, and the sound of five shots echoed through my mind. I realized these prisoners were part of the millions of Jews who were killed by the SS and their followers.

I asked Mama, "Did you know of these atrocities?"

"No, I didn't know, I didn't. I thought Flossenbuerg was for political and criminal prisoners. I was so worried and taken up with survival for my family and myself I didn't ask, nor did I wonder too much about anything of that nature. Even if I had, what would have happened? We learned a long time ago that anyone who opposed the Nazis or the SS openly went to prison. Now we know that dissidents were sentenced to the concentration camps and it was there where their resistance and their life ended. The world will judge us and say, 'We fault you, because you sat on your hands, and closed your eyes and ears.' We hear it already. I don't even know if Papa knew. He never discussed it with me."

Despite all the changes and turmoil, on August 29th, our baby boy, Werner, was born. "It wasn't an easy, smooth birth, so you will have to take over," Mrs. Rahn, the midwife, said. "Take the baby to the kitchen, keep him warm, and give him a few drops of warm water. I will come back after I am done with Peppi,"

I took the baby from Mama. As I stroked his tiny hand, I was shocked at how cold he felt on this hot August afternoon.

"These war babies need a lot of care," Mrs. Rahn explained. "Their circulation is slow, and most of them are small and below-average weight. It is a wonder they survive on what they have to grow on."

Resi came up to us. "Let me see him. He's my brother, too, you know." She cooed at him and remarked, "He's little, but we'll take care of him."

We had retrieved the crib and the box of little baby shirts and the soft linen diapers that Mama had saved after we had outgrown them. Resi centered our little brother on a huge diaper. Then she straightened his tiny legs and held them tight while I quickly pulled the left side of the diaper to the right and folded the bottom half up over his toes until it covered the baby's chest. I brought the remainder of the fold across the back and pinned the edges of the diaper securely to the left front. Resi and I had watched Mama when she swaddled Max and Irmgard, so we knew that a baby's legs grew straight and strong only if they were tightly swaddled. We washed an old pacifier in hot water, and moved it around the baby's lips until it started sucking.

Mrs. Rahn praised us. "You did a good job swaddling him. Watch your mama. She has no milk for the baby, so you will have to give him your milk rations and some water. Don't feed him during the night. He will cry, but the sooner he learns that he is not going to be fed, the sooner he will sleep all night."

During the evening hours Kenny walked through the gate and I called out, "Kenny, Mama . . . baby!" He rushed back to the Jeep driver and retrieved a small sack.

As we walked up to Mama, he handed her the sack. "For you," he said.

Surprised, she smiled weakly and said, "You open it?"

He opened the sack and he laid a bar of laundry soap on the down cover. He reached for more . . . several oranges, some crackers, packets of coffee, some egg powder, and a small box.

"Here," he said to Mama, "good for you."

Mama opened it and we stood in awe as aspirin tablets rolled onto the floor. We had not seen an aspirin for months. Kenny gathered the precious pills in his hand, bent down and gently hugged Mama.

"Thank you. Thank you," she whispered.

"All for you." Kenny patted her hands and he held them in his, until Mama broke the silence, "Want to hold the baby, Kenny?"

"Yes," he said as he reached for Werner.

A sound behind us made us turn and we froze. There stood Uncle Pepp. He was rubbing his eyes, but with gruffness in his voice he announced,

"I came to see Peppi. Heard it is a boy. Congratulation."

"Yes, it is." Mama said.

"Well, show that American a German boy. Go on."

Resi, Irmgard and I watched as Kenny looked at our baby and smiled.

"Nice boy." I laid the baby into Kenny's arms. He held it awkwardly and walked up to Uncle Pepp.

"He sure is little," Uncle Pepp said, "but, how can we raise big men without food? Peppi, you get some rest, we will keep Max and Irmgard with us, and I'll check back tomorrow or the next day. Now take care of everything."

Kenny, too, got up, and Uncle Pepp and Kenny walked out side by side.

CHAPTER TWENTY-SEVEN

CROSSING THE LINE

In a brief baptism ceremony at home, our baby brother was named Werner. Since Mama was still ill and didn't regain her strength, Resi and I took turns waiting in line at the distribution centers for our daily allotments of food. The main responsibility for Mamas and Werner's care, the struggle of providing food, and keeping house took its toll on me. One afternoon, I went to Uncle Pepp's bakery. It was late and the store had just closed, so I walked through the kitchen, into the pantry, and I stopped just before I entered the store. There, Louise Biedl and Uncle Pepp checked through a sack of vegetables from the greenhouse.

"OK, just what your papa and I agreed upon," Uncle Pepp offered. "Two loaves of snowy-white bread for the contents in the sack."

Louise smiled sweetly. "That will be fine, Mister Soelch." She gathered the bread into a huge sack, flung it over her shoulder, and left.

Surprised, Uncle Pepp looked at me, placed dark, crusty slices of bread on the counter and said, "You are late for your rations, but here they are."

I thought of Mama, her constant stomach aches, and the snowy-white loaves of bread I had just seen.

"No," I said and pushed the dark bread back. "I want snowy-white bread just like you gave Louise."

"Now why should I do that?" Uncle Pepp asked as he stepped toward me.

"Because you are my papa's brother. Mama gets sick when she eats those dark clumps of bread."

"Louise brought me vegetables, so what are you trading for?"

"Nothing, because I have nothing to trade. You know we barely survive."

"Nothing for nothing. Now take your bread and leave," Uncle Pepp commanded.

Tremors of fear rippled through me, but I couldn't back down now. I steeled myself against him, my head barely met his chest.

"I will not leave without white bread, and I will get white bread from now on — just for Mama until she is well."

Uncle Pepp pushed against me. "And if you don't get it? Tell me, what will you do?"

I braced myself against his chest and looked up, straight into his eyes. "If I don't get white bread any other way, by God, I'll turn you in for black marketing. Not just for today but I know you also traded illegally in the past."

Uncle Pepp's eyes pierced into mine, his face flushed to a deep red, he grabbed me by the front of my dress, lifted me off my feet and held me in his grip until my stare met the white of his eyes.

"You wouldn't do that to your father's brother, would you? You wouldn't dare!"

I was scared, but I said, my voice trembling, "If you make me, I will." As he put me down, I gained courage, "All I want is white bread for Mama. Resi, Max, Irmgard and I will eat whatever you bake, but not Mama. She can't. She needs white bread and she will have it if I can help it. Now, it is up to you."

Suddenly, he laughed and laughed as he regained his composure. "You had me going there, but just for a minute," he said. "If you were a man, I would watch you. You should have been a boy."

He reached for my sack, took the dark slices of bread that were still lying on the counter, and he replaced them with a loaf of snowy-white bread.

"Now take the bread and get home. From now on, just until your mother is well, see me for the bread. If I am not here, Erna will know what to give to you for Peppi. Now run along."

"Wait," he added. "Before you go, tell me the truth. You weren't serious, you wouldn't turn me in, not in a hundred years?"

I turned away from him and didn't answer. I could not let him see that I was shaking while tears were rolling down my hot, burning cheeks. My stomach protested, aching, turned in knots. I had the white bread so why did I feel so rotten?

All the way home, I was angry with myself and Uncle Pepp. Why does he always bring out the worst in me? I thought. Would I really have turned him in if he would have forced me to make good on my threat? I had no answer. I felt sick, and I felt such shame.

At home, as I approached Mama's bedroom I reasoned, "Maybe when I see Mama eating good, snowy-white bread I will feel better."

But Mama's reaction made me feel even worse. "Anneliese, whatever did you do to get white bread from Pepp? You two are at each other all the time. What did you trade off?" she asked.

"Nothing, Mama. Nothing is missing here," I murmured. "He just wanted to do the right thing for you."

After that, we always got snowy-white bread; but for me, it had a bitter taste. Whenever I ate it, I felt as if Uncle Pepp were looking at me, asking, "You wouldn't turn me in, would you?"

Still, I had no answer. Daily, the scene in the store played itself over and over in my mind, and I imagined how Uncle Pepp would get even with me. Would he turn me in for taking white bread from him? Would he tell Mama how I threatened him, or worse yet, was I destined to suffer in silence every time we met? These questions loomed before me when several days later Uncle Pepp and Grandma came by. My heart pounded and my cheeks flushed as I waited for Uncle Pepp's recall of how I had threatened him. But he never mentioned the bread incident, because he had other, more pressing problems on his mind.

"Peppi," he said, "If the Czechs close the East/West border within the next days Lisbeth will be cut off from West Germany, and her safety and future will be uncertain unless we act right now."

Grandma turned toward Mama and I thought her eyes were piercing right into my soul. "Do daughters ever do what a mother asks?" Without waiting for an answer she continued. "If Lisbeth had listened, she would not be in this terrible situation. Ever since February I have told her, Lisbeth, bring your furniture and all you can spare to Mitterteich. Don't wait! Pepp thinks the Czechs will take the Sudetenland back and it will become Czechoslovakia once more. When that happens you and your family must get out quickly and if you have your belongings here, you and Anton can start over. If things stay quiet, you can take your furniture back and nothing is lost. Anton, that all-knowing husband of hers, told me, 'We are not moving anything because I know we will be all right here. After all, the families we know are Germans and their ancestors lived here since the Middle Ages. What are the Czechs going to do, depeople the Sudetenland? Never, they need us, just like we need them.' Oh, he is such a Dummkopf."

"We hear rumors and half-truths, and they do nothing to disquiet the anxiety we feel," Uncle Pepp explained. "All we know for sure is the fact that Czechs from Bohemia, Moravia, and Slovakia have crossed into the Sudetenland, and they are seizing the homes of the Sudeten Germans. They have taken all able-bodied men for deportation and no one knows where they are, but we have heard from reliable sources that families have been forcefully marched off to work in the mines. The men were beaten, and they had to watch while their women, and girls barely fourteen, were raped by Czech men and boys. One of the sources said, 'I speak their language, so the Czechs took me for one of them. I couldn't watch any longer, but I didn't dare to leave. Even now I can hear the screams of the men, their women and their children. I will never forget what one man can do to another. Suicides are rampant. If they had caught me, I would have prayed for a bullet, but, most of the time, the Czechs weren't that kind. In Eger, near the border it is better, if you can call losing everything you ever had better. Before deportation, the Czechs tell everyone, 'You'll have fifteen minutes. Each family member can gather ten kilos of personal items. NO more! Then you must leave, and can never return, so get out while you can, or stay, and we ship you off to Russia.'"

Grandma shook her head. "How will Lisbeth fare with six-year-old Reserl, four-year-old George, and little Anton, barely two?"

"She is so isolated in Eger," Mama said. "Five miles from here, but she may as well be in another world for all we can do."

Imploringly, Uncle Pepp looked at me, "Anneliese, there is something you can do for me and your Aunt Lisbeth. We understand that your American Kenny drives into Eger?"

"Maybe he does. I know Captain Redman and he inspect the American check points along the border. So they must go to Eger,"

I surmised.

"We wondered," Uncle Pepp reflected, "if we gave him Lisbeth's address, maybe he could get in touch with her, or better yet, maybe he could bring some items across for Lisbeth? I saw the mayor this morning and while we were discussing the situations in Czechoslovakia, several American vehicles came back from Eger loaded with household appliances and furniture. Right then I thought of Kenny and how he could help Lisbeth." He paused and smiled. "Since Kenny doesn't speak German, I asked the mayor's secretary, who is fluent in English, to write this note."

Uncle Pepp handed the neatly folded note to me and continued, "We can't let Lisbeth down," he said. "She is your papa's and my sister, she is family."

"Pepp, if it is possible Kenny will help," Mama interrupted. "You will see, he is a good man. When he comes tonight, Anneliese will give him the note."

I wanted to hug Mama. She let Uncle Pepp and Grandma know what she thought of Kenny.

Grandma shook her head. "I still don't approve of your relationship with the American soldier, but Pepp reminded me that God works in mysterious ways. Maybe this was meant to be." She turned to Uncle Pepp. "We must get back, work is waiting at the bakery, but as soon Anneliese can tell us, we will make the necessary arrangements."

Mama followed them to the foyer while I stayed behind. I couldn't wait to scan the neatly penned note, but the foreign words revealed no more than Uncle Pepp had already told us. If Kenny can help, I reasoned, the slate between Uncle Pepp and myself should be clean. Right after Kenny's arrival, I handed him the note and we waited anxiously for his reply.

"Good English," he said. Then he shook his head, "Anneliese, C-Company must go to America, September 19. No more Eger. So sorry."

I looked helplessly at him, and then at Mama. Momentarily, the news he had so haltingly given sunk in. Kenny was leaving.

"No," I cried out as I reached for him.

He cupped my face in his hands. "Yes, Anneliese, I must go. C-Company in Tirschenreuth. I come back, tomorrow? Next day?"

He put his arms around me, while he spoke to Mama. "Mama, I must go back to America." Mama nodded and was silent.

My concern about Aunt Lisbeth's safety had faded and all I could think of was how could I go on without Kenny? No matter what happened during the day, when he came in the evening, everything was better, manageable. His smile and his easy-going manner had captivated my family and friends, and I had grown to love him.

"Mama" I said, "things won't be the same without Kenny."

"We will miss him, Anneliese. For now I will take Max and Irmgard for a short walk so you can spend time with Kenny before he leaves."

Kenny asked, "I walk back to Waldsassen. We go for walk?"

Usually we took the back roads, but tonight Kenny was looking for a ride, so we walked through town. Some people acknowledged my greeting but others walked silently by. On the outskirt of town, stately old chestnut and apple trees lined both sides of the highway and their intertwined branches gave shade and protection to weary travelers. Kenny and I had reached a high peak in the road when we met three German soldiers. The soldier in the middle had his head wrapped in dirty bandages, and he leaned on his comrades for support. As we passed, I heard their condemnation.

"So this is what we fought for. Our women throw themselves at American soldiers. They can't even wait until we come home. All for a chocolate bar, I bet."

Momentarily I felt ashamed, but then I felt anger. How could they judge me like that? They didn't know me, they didn't know Kenny, and I didn't know them. If I could explain, "I wasn't looking for an American soldier, it just happened!" But how could they understand?

Kenny looked at me. I knew he could guess the context of their remarks. "Anneliese, you OK?"

"Yes, Kenny."

Suddenly walking wasn't fun anymore. So much had happened today. I wondered how everything would end for Aunt Lisbeth, Kenny and me, and the German soldiers.

"I am going back, Kenny."

Kenny understood. Looking in both directions, he kissed me lightly, and he said, "See you tomorrow or the next tomorrow. Good night, I love you."

I longed for the solitude of my room, but Mama and Resi were waiting for me. "If we could help Lisbeth, we would," Mama said, "but there is no way anyone can risk going into the mayhem Pepp described. Let's go to sleep. . . if we can. Maybe tomorrow will be a better day."

Dreams, intermingled with Aunt Lisbeth, Kenny, Mama and Uncle Pepp running back and forth without any sense of direction, caused me to sleep fitfully. I was glad when I saw the early dawn breaking beyond the hills. The sound of muffled voices came from the kitchen, and I realized that Mama and Uncle Pepp were already discussing Kenny's restriction to quarters.

Uncle Pepp accepted the news with a shrug, and he planned. "Well, we just have to look the border over and see what can be done. Anneliese, maybe you and Erna can walk along the border and see what's going on. It would be less obvious than my presence with one of my men. You will go this afternoon," he concluded.

I was anxious to get back into Uncle Pepp's good graces, but Mama opposed the plan. "I will not send Anneliese to the border. Who knows what could happen to the girls, don't you think about that?"

"Peppi, Erna is sensible and she will not do anything that will demand a daring action. Between the two of them they will be all right," Uncle Pepp reasoned.

"Mama" I pleaded, "wouldn't you want help if you were in Aunt Lisbeth's place? Maybe we can't help, but we should try."

Uncle Pepp nodded. "She is right, Peppi. You know she is right?"

"I know, Pepp," Mama was quiet, thinking. "I will worry, but it must be done. Lisbeth is family and we must help. Anneliese, when you go along the border, look, just look. Don't talk with anyone until you are away from the border. I want your promise."

"Mama, we'll go along the border and look. That's all we will do."

"Wear the shabbiest dress you have, go barefoot, and no one will give you a second look," Uncle Pepp said. "Come around noon, you can eat with us, and then you will go along the border."

As Erna and I ate, Uncle Pepp gave final instructions. "Go up to the border by Muenchreuth, hitch a ride if you can, but, if need be, you can walk the eight miles. Stay a safe distance from the crossing, but talk with people who are crossing over. First, ask when they think the border will close for good, and then ask what kind of papers are necessary to get across. I will try for information here. Now remember what I told you. Be careful."

We walked briskly past small villages, on to Muenchreuth when Erna, who had been silent, finally said, "Anneliese, why do you always get me into trouble? I really don't want to do this, not even for Aunt Lisbeth. Look around you, aren't you scared? When Papa tells me that you have more courage in your little finger than I have in my whole body, I don't care. I am angry, and I am hurt."

"Erna, why are you angry with me? Your papa asked Mama if I could go, so here I am."

"All my life, no one ever asked me what I want," she said. "Why am I here, where I don't want to be?" Erna lowered her head. "Let's get this over with, and as Papa said, let's stay together."

The beauty of the day, the sun warming the earth below our bare feet, the leaves of the trees rustling softly in the wind, and small birds flying above us belied the scenes below. As we neared the sparsely guarded East/West border, we saw people sitting in road ditches looking or waiting for loved ones. Deported families came across with their baggage and knapsacks half empty. Children cried from being overtired and confused, and adults wept because they were leaving their past, their homes, and even their loved ones behind.

"Barely a hundred pounds for all of us, that's what we have to start over. If you take anymore, or if you try to go back over the border, they shoot to kill. Where are we going; where will we start?" a woman cried out.

Erna and I carefully inched closer to the American check point. Across from us, Czech soldiers checked throngs of people they had forced to leave. Having reached the last stop before crossing, they wanted to get through as quickly as possible. No one pushed or shoved because the Czech guards were heavily armed and they seemed to enjoy their job.

"How does it feel to have nothing?" one soldier asked no one in particular. Hearing that, Erna and I grew fearful for our safety, but we feared much more for the man with the rusty, old bike. He stood near the hut of the Czech check point, and he was pleading to keep his bike.

"I need my bike to get around. You have everything else I ever owned. I will not give you my bike. Never!", he cried out.

The soldier tried to take it, but the man resisted and would not give up. Suddenly, their confrontation elevated to shoves and angry shouts and they became the single focus point. Suddenly, the soldier untied the leather whip from his Army coat, extended his arm, lifted the whip, cracked it skillfully into the air and brought it down until the upper part of the whip ensnared the man's neck. The force buckled the man's knees under, but he clung to his bike as he fell to the ground. Again, the soldier gyrated the whip upward until it circled above his head; then swaying rhythmically, he cracked the whip across the man's back again . . . and again. With each blow, screams pierced the air; and with each scream the whip's speed increased and finally it fell aimlessly across the man's body until he lay still, coiled into a fetal position, bleeding.

Transfixed, people from the East and West watched as the soldier unfastened the saber from his belt. I covered my eyes, and turned away, expecting death. But the sound that followed was not a scream, it was the sound of someone ripping a cloth. I couldn't understand it. Through my spread fingers, I saw the soldier standing there, slashing his own coat into strips. He placed his booted feet on the sides of the man's body, and bowed down. Methodically, he tied the strips of his coat around the bleeding hands and arms of the man he had just whipped.

Erna put her head on my shoulder, then she slid into the nearby ditch and heaved. "Oh God, oh God, " she gasped.

We heard an ambulance with its siren wailing, bearing down the road. Still stunned, everyone moved quietly aside while an American driver and an attendant had angry words with the Czech guards. The driver signaled, and with lightning speed, the Americans pulled the bleeding man across the border barriers. He cried out in pain as they gently lifted him into the ambulance and closed the doors with somber determination. Some people knelt and prayed, others watched in stony silence until the ambulance with its sirens screaming, sped away.

A soldier picked up the bike and leaned it against the Czech's guard hut. People talked in murmurs, moved slowly toward the border barriers, and checked out.

Erna sat on the ground. Her hair looked fiery red against her ashen skin.

I asked, "Erna, are you all right?"

She held her hand over her chest, "Never, ever will I be all right. Oh, God, oh God," she cried while her teeth chattered and her body trembled violently. Shaken and afraid I sat down next to her. I stroked her hair while she whimpered and I stared into space.

Erna finally said, "Let's go home, I can't stand it here."

"Erna, if we can, we should ask questions of the deportees. Maybe we can ask them on the way home."

It seemed everyone who had been on the West side felt the need to leave. The road to Waldsassen was teeming with deportees who carried their possessions on their backs. Some were silent while others were eager to relive the past days and hours.

A woman told us what she knew. "I heard it will take another month or so before the Czechs close the border. They are determined to deport all Germans and bring their own people and the Gypsies to settle the Sudetenland. This morning their soldiers came at the crack of dawn, and they gave us fifteen minutes to pack. We are lucky to be here, though, near Prague. Further into Czechoslovakia, I heard they clubbed our wounded soldiers to death and the field hospitals became places of carnage." She cried silently for several minutes while we groped for consoling words, but we found none.

Another woman reflected, "I don't even know if I took the right items. What can you take in fifteen minutes? I couldn't think. It would have been better if the house had been bombed out. It was so hard to just walk out and leave a lifetime of living behind. We had worked for years, and now we are reduced to beggars. I hope that we can sleep in barns until we get to my sister. She has a bombed-out family living with them, but she will make room. Until a few days ago, I thought we were the lucky ones, the ones who survived the war."

Erna and I walked straight to the bakery and relayed what we had heard. Uncle Pepp listened, and then he pensively shook his head and asked, "We heard a that a Czech soldier mercilessly whipped an old man over a rusty bike?"

Neither Erna nor I wanted to talk about the brutal whipping we had just witnessed. I cried out. "I want to forget the flying whip, the screams, and the old man wrenching in pain. So don't ask me about it, not ever again!"

Mama was relieved to see me. "Anneliese, you have done your part. I'm glad it is over. Peter, the interpreter, stopped by and he said that Kenny will see you when he can."

On the evening of the eighteenth of September, Kenny came early.

"Tonight last time I can come. C-company in Tirschenreuth ...Mama, I came to say good-bye," Kenny explained.

Kenny had gifts for everyone: The gum and candy were special treats for Max and Irmgard, and Resi loved the soaps he had for her, but they were sad and distraught as they hugged for the last time.

Then he reached for his camera. "You take pictures," he said. Blurry eyed, I clicked away until Kenny was satisfied. He took the film and said, "My family from Germany."

"Anneliese," Mama said, "I don't know if I am doing the right thing, but Kenny has been so good to us. I know you want to give him something special before he leaves." She handed me Papa's ruby ring. "Take it and give it to Kenny. I know he will think of us, but I imagine he will mainly think of you."

The gold band with its scroll design around the small ruby glistened in my hand. "Mama, I hope Papa won't mind. I know that Kenny will treasure this beautiful ring."

"Now if you want to walk with Kenny to Tirschenreuth, go ahead."

I thanked Mama for giving us these extra hours when Kenny and I could be alone. I knew I would keep the ring until the last minute because it is meant for a special time.

As everyone said their final good-byes, Max, Irmgard and Resi told Kenny, "Come back and live here."

Mama took her leave. With tears flowing down his cheeks, Kenny held her tightly. "Mama, thank you. You are my family, always."

When everyone had left, I took the ring from the envelope

and offered it to Kenny. "This is Papa's. Now yours. Don't forget us."

Kenny haltingly explained, "Anneliese. You are mine. I'll not forget you. Never." Our kisses sealed the promise. Kenny pushed me gently away. "We must go. Seven miles to Tirschenreuth, a long walk back for you, Anneliese."

The night air was cool. The blue night sky was speckled with stars, and the harvest moon illuminated the hills, meadows, and homes along the street. We avoided the painful present while we hoped for times when the world wouldn't look at us as enemy aliens, but as two people who loved each other. We passed small lakes stocked with Christmas carps. Thick tendrils of rising fog hid the croaking frogs, and the woods on both sides of the road filled the air with heavy pine scent. The outline of Tirschenreuth came into view and our hearts grew heavy.

"Anneliese, we say good-bye here, not Tirschenreuth." Kenny said.

"No, I will walk with you to the train."

As we approached the dilapidated box-cars, the military police told Kenny that I couldn't go any further. His comrades waved, and they were calling to Kenny. "Come, come on, we leave! Kiss her good-bye!"

The wheels of the train started to grind and someone gave the final boarding call. We embraced once more and I said, "Auf Wiedersehen, Kenny!"

I turned from him. Kenny ran for the train and the hands of his comrades reached out and lifted him up into the box-car. I waved until the train became a spot in the distance. "Auf Wiedersehen, Kenny!" I whispered, and slowly I turned away.

CHAPTER TWENTY-EIGHT

1945 — 1947 COPING

Just then, Peter, the C-Company's interpreter stopped his jeep and called out, "Anneliese, hop in, Kenny said that I should watch out for you and take you home."

All too soon I found that life without Kenny was not easy. His presence in the evenings made the struggles for existence more tolerable for me and my family as well. But now, our hopes for a better life diminished more with each day. Insufficient food rations were not always available so we searched for food substitutions in the fields and woods were we picked mushrooms and blue berries, and we dig in the fields for potatoes and sugar beets the farmers left behind. We cooked the sugar beets, and their sickly sweet smell penetrated throughout the homes and stayed on for days after we mashed the pulp and saved the syrup as sweetener. Refugees poured in from East Germany and the Sudentenland, and they were housed in the barracks where once the foreign labor workers had lived. No one had more to live on than their daily rations, and the factories were still.

We knew that Christmas 1945 would come and go like any other day — the only gift we had was being together as a family. What Mama and I wanted most was a sign of life from our men but it did not happen. Every week I walked ten miles to Waldassen hoping I would receive a letter from Kenny, but so far, I always returned empty handed. All the while Mama and all of us waited for Papa to return to his family. We hoped he had survived the war, and we longed for him to come home. Uncle Pepp looked out for us, but I did not relish his visits because he always asked,

"Well, what do you hear from Kenny?" He knowingly nodded, "Well, no mail? Peppi, maybe now Anneliese will come to her senses."

Finally, I received letters from Kenny. He still wanted nothing more than to be with me. During August 1946, Max came running and he pointed to a man, "He knows where Papa is! He knows."

The man before us personified the prisoners of war he had seen during the past months. His eyes were dull and sunken, his skin was grayish-white, his features were bloated and his skin was covered with sores that didn't heal. Yet, he had a quiet dignity about him, and I was ready to believe the news he would share with us. He reached in his pocket and wordlessly handed Mama a photo postcard. At first she read it silently, and then, with every muscle drawn and tears streaming down her face she shared Papa's message with us.

Pularvij (Poland), September 8, 1945

Dear Peppi,

It has been such a long time since I could get in touch with you and assure you that I am still well and I am among the living. I was taken as a prisoner of war by the Russians on March 3, 1945.

The Russians do not give us an opportunity to get in touch with anyone. Maybe you have already considered the possibility that I may be among the dead, but we will see each other again. I am counting on it; Hopefully, I will come home to you and the children and I pray that I will find you well. I haven't heard from you since we parted in Neustetting. The burden that we must carry now is bitter and hard, but we will survive. Keep your head high, dearest Peppi, The main thing right now is that we have escaped death and injury. Even thought we survive naked and barely living and it is an indescribably hellish time, we must thank God. Now, dear Peppi, I hope these lines will get to you and find you well and at home. I long for you and God willing, we will be together soon. My love and kisses to you and the children, always, your Max.

Papa's Photo Postcard - Papa, third man seated from the right.

We were thankful to hear from papa, but now we felt his absence deeply, and we could not stop our tears. The man told us that he had met Papa in Berlin where they lived in a bombed-out home until the Russians found them. They were herded onto trucks with Lithuanians, Poles, women and even children while their caravan trekked on — to Russia. "Max and I told each other that whoever would come home first would get in touch with the family. Max hid his cards in the lining of his cap, and he gave it to me before the Russians took him away.

"We heard through the camp grapevine that Max and others were taken to build roads in Siberia. The camp was hellish as he said. When the Russians released me and others, we feared their pent up anger so we banded together. We had no survival gear, we just had the rags on our backs. At the end of May we reached the border and the Russians let me cross, but they refused others to go through. At gunpoint they forced our men to kneel down and crawl like dogs. I watched in horror while they groveled in the dirt and on command begged and cried for release or death. Then with freedom ten steps away, the Russian guards dragged our men back in the waiting trucks and shipped the men I had befriended back to inland Russia to become prisoners of war once again." The man broke down, and cried, unashamed. Then he went on.

"Now that I have kept my promise to Max, I must go on and search for my family. We had a farm in Czechoslovakia, I hope my family got out."

"M'am," the man said, "All Max and I ever wanted was to be with our families, is that too much to ask?" He got up, and we bid each other farewell.

Now that we knew where Papa was, we feared for his safety and every day we prayed that he would come home to us. I too, prayed that I would soon be reunited with Kenny. In his letters he told me that he still loved me, and he was waiting for me to come to America. Mama relaxed because until now she had not believed that I could ever gain permission to emigrate to America and marry Kenny. I had applied several times for a visa or Exit Permit, but I had never received an answer from the American Consulate. Now, Mama was in shock, and she called for Uncle Pepp's help shortly after Congressman Hagen sent me a copy of the letter he had written to the Consul at Munich, Bavaria.

Congress of the United States
House of Representatives
Washington, D.C.

January 22, 1947

American Consul
Munich, Germany

Dear Sir:

> RE: Anneliese Soelch
> Application for visa

I have been working with Mr. Kenneth Woodstrom for several months in connection with his case and we are both very much discouraged over the fact that so little progress has been made. At this time I want to assure you that I am personally acquainted with Kenneth Woodstrom. I know his family well and their financial status and I have personal knowledge of his intent to marry Anneliese Soelch on her arrival in the United States.

I also live in Crookston, Minnesota and am particularly anxious that this case be brought to a speedy and favorable conclusion.

Sincerely yours,

Harold C. Hagen
U.S. Rep. in Congress

My happiness knew no bounds. Now Mama, Uncle Pepp, and everyone in my family knew that Kenny had been true to me and that we had a chance of gaining permission to marry. I kept working with the counsel in Munich, and after the letter from Congressman Hagen, everything fell into place, and finally, Kenny and I would soon be together.

CHAPTER TWENTY-NINE

WITHER THOU GOEST...I WILL GO

It had been eighteen months since Kenny and I had said our final good-byes in Tirschenreuth. Now it was Maundy Thursday, April 2, 1947. All day long onto past midnight, acquaintances, relatives, and friends had stopped by to bid me farewell. Their laughter while we reminisced, the brief silence when words would not come, and the pain of their last embraces lingered while I stood by the garden gate and watched until the curve in the road had swallowed up my friends' shadows. Dense ground mist lay thick upon the brook as the fog rose and clawed its way into the meadows. The velvet-blue night sky was studded with stars and the moon's brightness slowly exposed the distant hills where the tall, ancient fir trees had been veiled in inky-night blackness. The thought of tomorrow when I would leave this beautiful valley pressed in on me, but before I could succumb to sadness Mama came toward me. I wished that I could embrace Mama, but I knew it would cause too much hurt after all we had been through today. Tonight, Mama looked shorter than her stature of five feet and older than forty-three. Her blond, baby-fine hair was combed back but a few stubborn strands had separated from the clips and hung loosely onto her forehead. Swollen, red-rimmed eyelids paled her azure eyes, and tightly drawn face muscles made her face look even more gaunt than it had been of late. Her rounded shoulders bent forward but her movements showed sheer determination to stay in control.

"Anneliese, come, we need to sleep before morning."

I followed her into the kitchen where my sisters, Resi, sixteen; Irmgard, eight; and my brother Max, twelve; sat around the table with their eyes fixed on me as they waited. I felt uneasy as Mama's whisper broke the silence.

"It has been a long day with so many people bidding farewell, and in the morning we'll face another hard day so let's go to bed." Before we could respond, she rose and turned toward me, "Anneliese, I moved Baby Werner. It is best for you that he sleeps in my room. Good night, everyone, sleep well."

Hastily, Resi, Ma˘, and Irmgard mumbled good night and scrambled past Mama before she closed the door. Left alone the familiar night noises of the house unsettled me, so I fled to my room and stepped in the void that a few hours ago had held Baby Werner's crib. Since Mama had never fully recuperated after Werner's birth, he had slept in my room. His absence, the bare walls, empty closets and bookshelves shattered my sureness. Wanting to forget momentarily what lay ahead of me, I undressed, climbed into bed, and as I had done thousands of times, I snuggled under my down covers and hoped for sleep. But, sleep would not come since the grinding thump of Mama's restlessness denied me sleep. I could picture her as she walked back and forth the length of her bedroom. One, two, thump thump, the floor boards creaked methodically. In want of medication, she stamped her feet while she tried to cope with the arthritic pain that robbed her of the rest she so desperately needed.

"Please, God, not now. Don't let Mama's legs hurt tonight," I prayed.

Suddenly, the thumping stopped, and within minutes Mama entered my room. She closed the door quietly behind her and turned on the light.

I feigned deep sleep, but Mama shook me and said, "Anneliese, you are not sleeping. Open your eyes. We need to talk."

"Mama," I pleaded, "please, turn off the light. We can talk in the morning."

"No! We have four hours left, so you listen and don't you shut me out!" she reprimanded. She took my face into her hands and made me look at her. "Anneliese, even as a baby you seemed to have your own way of doing things and making up your mind. You always flew before you knew how you would land. Now you are flying to America where you will marry Kenny whom you have known for twelve short weeks."

"But Mama, you like Kenny and you know he is good man."

Despairing, Mama continued. "Anneliese, there are millions of good men. Why do you have to marry one from America? You don't speak English; Kenny doesn't speak German, Have you thought about the conflicts you will have to face? For the Americans you are an 'Enemy Alien' and you will encounter families who lost their fathers or sons in Germany. Ask yourself, what will they feel toward you? Love? You are a Roman Catholic; Kenny is a Lutheran. Will you be able to change your faith and join the church where Kenny's brother-in-law is a minister? I don't think you can do it. Kenny is ten years older than you and you will live with his parents. Tell me, Anneliese, how will you cope? The fact that you think you can solve all these problems, or that they will just melt away once you are married, tells me that you are not prepared for marriage."

"Mama, we love each other. We will work together and resolve our differences fairly," I answered. .

"That sounds like something you read in a romance story, but remember, in real life nothing is fifty-fifty in a marriage. What worries me is that for the past eighteen months you have refused consistently to face the consequences of your decision."

"I know what I am doing!"

"You don't," said Mama. "Do you realize what you are giving up? Even our soldiers said that homesickness can be like a slow death, and they were with their comrades." Mama cried out, "You will be alone in a strange land with people you have never met. Who will console you when you are homesick, who will advise you when you need help?"

"Kenny and I will make it!" I knew my trembling voice did little to convince her.

Despairingly, Mama pleaded. "Anneliese, for once, listen to me! After tomorrow, we can not talk like we always have. You will be over eight thousand miles from home."

"We can write to each other."

"Letters from America will take months to reach me," she cried out. "You haven't heard a word I have said. If Papa was here, he could make things right. He always could. What will he do when he comes home from the Russian Prisoner of War Camp and learns that you are married to an American soldier? He doesn't know Kenny, so it will not be easy for him to accept that you left us to marry an enemy soldier. I will be here to face his disappointment and his anger. Just how much do you ask of me? How much do you think I can take?"

Mama's pleading outburst frightened me so I remained silent. Suddenly, Mama gripped my shoulders and shook me with an intensity I didn't know she possessed.

"You don't have an answer for that! Do you?" she snapped. And with that she slapped me until my cheeks stung, and my limbs trembled. I reached up to protect my face and Mama stopped hitting me.

Gasping for breath, she lamented, "What have I done? Dear God, please, help me! What can I do to make her understand all that lies ahead?"

She looked at the palms of her hands and brought them up until they covered her face, and she wept. Each labored breath she took invaded my body and it protested in pain. As her sobbing waned, she sat inert on the edge of my bed while the room seemed to press in on us. Finally, she sighed and shook her head. "Nothing works. I can see you have decided, so what is there left for me to do but wish you the best."

Mama leaned down and hugged me. She moaned, kissed me, and blessed me with drops of Holy Water that she kept in a miniature stoup near each bedroom door.

Crossing herself, she prayed, "Please, God, take care of her. I can't do any more for her." She sighed wearily and left the room as suddenly and quietly as she had entered.

I was glad Mama didn't hear the sobs that racked my body. She had succeeded. Her words had diminished my confidence and her slapping me had shaken my whole being. I could not recall her ever slapping me so hard. Fear of what lay ahead gripped me; I wished for time to stand still so that tomorrow would never come. Too spent to move, I finally fell into a troubled sleep until the rays of the bright morning sun warmed my cheeks, and a blast of cool, fresh air swept into my room.

Resi had opened the windows and fastened them to the hook on the window frame.

"Good morning, Anneliese," she said, as she threw back her shoulders and stood up straight. "Mama said you need to get up now."

As children, Resi and I had vied for Mama and Papa's attention. It wasn't easy for me to compete because Resi kept everything neat and she knew intuitively how to stay out of trouble. I was convinced she was Mama's favorite because she always got whatever she wanted without waiting for the right age and Mama and Papa always excused her from household chores because she was the little one. During the war years our childish competition ceased. We developed common interests, watched out for each other, and shared our hopes and dreams.

"Resi," I whispered, and I held out my arms. She came to me.

"I miss you already," she cried out. "We have become friends and now you leave me. What will I do without you?"

"I wish you could come with me." My voice broke, I could say no more and neither could she.

Resi released herself from my embrace. "It is almost six. Mama said that you should get up now. You'll have to leave for the depot by nine o'clock."

I procrastinated while I washed and dressed, and thought all the while of the long, scary journey ahead of me. I fetched my shoes. The uppers were thin, wrinkled and scuffed leather, and the inch-thick, wooden soles had withstood many repairs. Four weeks earlier I had gone to the town hall to seek the necessary stamped approval for new shoes. The town clerk listened to my request and responded, "I don't know, Fraulein Solch, I'd better ask the mayor about that."

"The mayor?" I gasped in disbelief.

"Yes," he reiterated as the mayor stepped forward.

"So, Fraulein Solch, you have permission to enter America and you want a permit for new shoes?"

"Yes," I stammered inaudibly. Gradually I gathered courage, and I pleaded, "Mister Mayor, my shoes are six years old and beyond repair. Mama wore them before she handed them down to me. I need new shoes."

The mayor's tone was serious. "I hope you do understand why I cannot sign. We have so many applicants with priority permits, yet we never receive enough shoes to fill every request. Fraulein Solch, in America there is no shortage of anything. If you have the money, you can buy a pair of shoes there...." he paused and snapped his fingers, "just like that! America is a land of plenty, and we have nothing here."

He stepped toward me and cordially bid me goodbye. "Auf Wiedersehen, Fraulein Solch, the best to you in your new life. God be with you."

After that visit, whenever I looked at my shoes, I wondered if the mayor was right. Could anyone in America get shoes without a permit and without waiting for years?

I looked at Grandma's battered wicker suitcase which now held trousseau, and a few gifts, all that I owned. We had worked hard to assemble the wardrobe for my journey. Resi and I had ripped three patched sweaters and for days we had unraveled yarn, designed patterns and knitted. Now I owned two new sweaters. We re-dyed my blue suit until the dye hid the shiny worn spots and the old hemline. Since we lacked soap or bleach, we laid an old bed sheet on the grass in our yard and relied on nature to bleach the fabric. Resi's sewing skills turned the bleached bed sheet into a blouse.

Kenny had left an American army blanket. Mama was sure that with sufficient dye and water the blanket could be made into a coat. Friends and neighbors donated from their daily water rations and we boiled the blanket in a dye solution. After several treatments, the khaki army blanket finally was the right shade of black. Our tailor cut the blanket into a fashionable princess style coat.

The sound of the doorbell interrupted my reminiscing, and I heard the booming voice of Uncle Pepp.

Frequently, I had heard him sounding gruffer than he was today. "Well, where is the bride?" he asked. "Has she changed her mind, or is she still leaving us? Here, I brought some bread from the bakery, and I won't ask for any of your ration stamps because this is on me. Not really, someone on the black market will just get less tonight. After a while we'll eat, but first, I must see the bride and give her fatherly advice."

Hearing that remark, I hastily I entered the kitchen and steeled myself for his inquisition. He greeted me. "Good morning, Sleepy Head. You will have to change your ways: wives don't sleep late, they cook breakfast in the morning, and they serve their husbands. I always say a man has to lay down the law."

I remained silent. Uncle Pepp changed his tactics. "Well, are you ready to fly over the big ocean? You know, I could have found you a man here, but no, you have to go to America. If you married a Berliner, or someone from the North, I could explain such a marriage to your Papa. But why you want an American, that defies reason."

I tried to appease him. "Papa would want me to be happy. I will write to him, and Mama will talk with him and explain."

"Explain?" Uncle Pepp went on. "How can we explain that there was no man good enough for you here? You wouldn't go anywhere with Franz, or Heinz, good Bavarian boys they are. What was the matter with them, tell me?"

"Pepp," Mama retorted, "breakfast is ready, and just for today, we will eat in peace."

Uncle Pepp took his place at the head of the table and said. "Let us give thanks. After all, this bread is a gift from the Lord. Max, quit staring at the bread, bow your head, and close your eyes."

Uncle Pepp led us in prayer. "Thank you, Lord, for the gift of bread you provided. Bless us, and please, keep Anneliese in your grace. We beseech you, Lord look after her. We tried, but we failed. Now she will need you, more than ever. Amen." He turned to Max. "Now you may eat."

We ate our rations in silence until Mama cautioned. "We must leave soon. We have a twenty minute walk to the depot. Anneliese, say good-bye to Max."

So far, twelve-year-old Max took my leaving for America as a big adventure. I loved him deeply because he always was all boy and much to Mama's consternation, he would roam outdoors for hours. Barefooted and alone he waded in the shallow brook on the outskirts of town, searched for treasures in the sand pits and muddy ponds, and filled his pockets with frogs and stones. When he tired of the waters, he explored the wooded hills. Max brought home hurt birds, insects, worms — anything he could hide in his pockets or under his jacket.

Now, he came toward me, faced me squarely, and reminded me, "Anneliese, don't you forget to send me a new soccer ball like you said you would."

I ruffled his flaxen hair affectionately. "Be good in school and if you behave for Mama, you may have a new soccer ball sooner than you think," I promised.

His blue eyes sparkled, and his smile revealed his anticipated pleasure. Beaming, he turned to Irmgard. "You'll see, I will have a brand-new soccer ball before you know it."

Since Irmgard was born in October 1939, she suffered from malnutrition. Almost daily Mama or I checked her skinny body, her sore arms, and her blotchy face, and wondered if the marks of impetigo would ever completely disappear. Her clothes and toys had always been hand-me-downs. She had never known peace nor the joy of owning something new.

Encouraged by Max's infectious enthusiasm, Irmgard sang out eagerly,

"You know that am Kenny's Second Lady. He said so when he brought me bandages and medicine when I had impetigo. I would like some food, a doll and a new coat. You will send it to me, won't you, Anneliese?" she asked snuggling up against me.

"The same rules for you, little lady. It all depends on how well you behave."

"Oh, I am always good, aren't I, Mama?"

"Yes, you little 'Miss Goody'. Now give Anneliese a hug and a kiss, then go upstairs where Mrs. Dimpfl is waiting for you and Max. Watch for the train, and when it comes by, you can wave to Anneliese."

Max came toward me and extended his right hand, but I reached for him and cupped his face in my hands.

"Be good, Max. Help Resi and Mama until Papa comes home."

He nodded while tears trickled on his shirt. I hugged him until he squirmed uneasily and slipped out of my embrace.

I reached for Irmgard. Kneeling next to her I caressed her skinny arms. "Irmgard, don't forget me. Remember, I love you." I couldn't say anymore, so I just held her tight.

Uncle Pepp urged, "Come, you two. Mrs. Dimpfl is in the foyer waiting for you."

Resi came in with Baby Werner. She had dressed him in his best sweater and she had combed his blond curls with extra care. Oblivious of what lay ahead, he came to me, he hugged me; he wanted to play. I cradled him against my chest while sobs jolted my rib cage. Baby Werner didn't understand my sudden crying. He struggled to free himself, but I couldn't let him go.

"Mama, I won't go without him. Please, let him come to the depot with me."

"No, Anneliese, that just can not be," she said firmly.

I locked my arms tightly around Baby Werner's tiny waist and wailed.

"I have taken care of him his whole life! Please let him come, let him see the train, I can't go without him. Why won't you do this small favor for me? Tomorrow, it will be too late, I will be gone!"

Mama stood still, she shook her head and sobbed without restraint while Resi stood helplessly by looking at Uncle Pepp. With tears in his eyes Uncle Pepp took over.

"Now, now, Anneliese, don't take it so hard. Give him to me, he will be all right. He will watch from upstairs."

He stroked my hair, gently took Werner from me and muttered as he left for upstairs, "Women, who can understand them?"

Within a few minutes he returned and so did his usual gruff manner as he barked directions at me. "Anneliese, you fetch your suitcase, and I will carry it. Your Mama and I thought that Erna should travel to Frankfurt with you, and she is waiting at the depot. Now mind you, don't put any of your wild notions in Erna's head. I won't give permission to a daughter of mine to leave for America and marry someone over there. I won't have it! Erna will marry Hans, a good Bavarian. One Solch girl leaving home is enough."

"Don't you worry about Erna, she won't leave home," I reassured him.

Mama interrupted. "We must leave."

She held out her arms. Mama's tears mingled with mine. I felt her anguish and I thought my heart could burst with pain as we hugged silently and held onto each other. I wanted to tell her once more how much I loved her, but I knew, if I did, I could not leave her.

Resi touched my shoulder, her eyelids red and her pupils clouded by tears. Before I could embrace her she moved toward the door. "I will write to you. Take care. I can't see you off!" she cried out as she closed the door behind her.

Uncle Pepp stepped toward me while he raised his arm and brushed the sleeve of his loden jacket over his cheeks. "I guess it is too late to tell you not to go. I hope those Americans know what they are getting. Kenny will have his hands full." He hugged me and muttered, "I just don't understand it; I never will." He paused, "I wish that Max were here, but he isn't, so let's get on the way."

As we left the house, I looked back at the place that was my home. Uncle Pepp pushed me gently. "Go," he urged. "You will see the house again from the train, and you can wave to everyone then. Anyway, don't take leaving so hard. I bet a hundred marks, Anneliese, in two years you will come to your senses, you will ask me for money so you can come home. Come to think of it, I will not send the money unless you promise you will come home to stay."

"Pepp, quit your badgering," Mama snapped. "Keep peace with Anneliese."

"I wish Resi were here to see me off."

"Remember, she usually disappeared when Papa left for a long-term job. She just can't say good-bye to the ones she loves," Mama concluded.

As we neared the depot, Uncle Pepp said, "Look at those people, they waited for you."

A group of elders stood aside talking to each other, while a young couple came up to me and asked, "We heard that you are going to America. Are you getting married there?"

Several bystanders called out, "Good luck."

"I wish I could go with you," said Mister Braun, who was at least fifty years old. "My mother's relatives are over there, somewhere. What is there here for us? Over there at least there is hope."

Cousin Erna, who had been talking with relatives and acquaintances, came toward us and said, "The gate to the train is open, Anneliese, we must board."

There was an almost festive atmosphere as we exchanged final hugs. Everyone, family and strangers as well, shouted farewell wishes while they waved good-bye with their white handkerchiefs. The same scene repeated itself as the train passed by my home. Erna and I stood by the window. The little ones, friends, and neighbors shouted and waved until their familiar voices died in the distance, their silhouettes faded into small specks and then nothingness.

Erna sat down and read, but I could not concentrate so I looked at the countryside in its spring beauty. During the early morning hours the cloudless blue sky, tucked in and held tightly by a border of hills, arched high over the tall pines, century old evergreens and scrawny silver birches. The villages nestled in the foothills with their slate-roofed farm houses, tall church steeples, sprawling meadows and small fields were familiar to me, and I didn't mind the whistle stops every five to ten miles because I knew all this beautiful scenery would not continue more than fifty miles. Then, the change of scenery, change of atmosphere, and change of people would be imminent.

Erna came up to me. "Anneliese," she pleaded, "you are only twenty years old, yet, you leave us. Think about it — come back with me — and wait until your papa comes home?"

"Papa isn't here, so leave him out of it, Erna," I pleaded. "Don't you start in on me, too. Everyone tells me what to do. First, it was wait six months, then wait a year, and for the past month Mama and your papa have not given me a moment's peace. Believe me, they have pointed out again and again the problems I could encounter in America."

"Anneliese, they only want the best for you. What will happen to you in America? I heard most people over there hate us because their sons and husbands have been killed or wounded on our soil. I bet they believe you are one of the Nazis who did terrible things to the Jews. We have just lost the war to the Americans. Do you really think they will welcome you with open arms?"

"Erna, I was thirteen years old when the war started and our families never were Nazis," I refuted. "I am going, and I won't come back, at least not for a long time. Your papa gave me two years, and he bet a hundred marks that I'll be back. Well, I say, 'Never! I'd sooner die first!'"

Erna looked shaken. "You have been through so much today, just come back when you can," she said softly.

"Erna," I pleaded, "look out there! What do you see? What could be worse than what we've been through the past eight years? The war was horrible, unthinkable. The past two years of occupation haven't been easy either. I think I've gained the strength to withstand anything."

We both fell silent as the foothills of the Fichtelgebirge fell behind us. The wheels of the train grated over the worn-out tracks and sparks spewed as we reached Nuremberg. The train stopped near mountainous debris that four years ago had been the railroad station. Instantly, we were engulfed by moving masses and we pushed and shoved until we found an empty platform space. Dreading the layover, we hid our luggage behind our backs, huddled to keep warm and watched. Children, women and men, stood, sprint ready, as they looked and pointed down the trodden path where an American patrol turned the corner. At will, they flipped cigarettes and cigarette butts in the watchers' direction. The Americans talked, laughed and shook their heads at the spectacle they had created. The watchers sprinted forward until they spied a cigarette landing near them. Within a flash, they threw themselves on the ground, pushing, and fighting until someone rose, arms raised, jumping joyfully and clutching their treasure while their friends cheered. Erna and I knew that cigarettes were sometimes better than money. With a good barterer, enough cigarettes could sustain the hungry or sick. We watched silently as men traded seven cigarettes for a pound of flour. Another group traded for water, and while the hunger-driven sat and salivated, their chosen leader mixed the flour with water until he held a lumpy dough. Eager hands pulled the dough into sheets that hardened none too soon for lucky owners. No one took chances with theft; they devoured the finished product and the hunger pains were stilled for now.

Near us crude scaffolds covered with scribbled messages and weather-beaten pictures of soldiers, children, and families were the meeting places for refugees, the KLV children, and all the other survivors of the war. These messages and pictures were the lost and found network of Germany's twentieth century's mayhem and madness.

We were overwhelmed by the constant motion that surrounded us. Dressed in tattered clothes, which were probably all they owned, bedraggled hollow-eyed homeless walked by looking for a space where they could perhaps stay for a few hours, or maybe a night. Others searched for a familiar face, or someone who might know the whereabouts of missing family members, friends, or acquaintances. Groups of people groped through the rubble for anything that could keep them warm. The most pitiful sight was the refugees. They had lost their homes which had been built by their ancestors centuries ago. Torn apart for the past four years by the ravages of war, families still huddled on their wagons or on the ground. Their nomadic life had taken its toll, and there was no end to the misery that surrounded us.

Disbelieving, we stared at bands of German soldiers who had withstood years of fighting on all fronts and were now clad in ill-fitting shirts, pants, and jackets. Some had lost their limbs, their hearing, or their sight. The more fortunate ones still had shoes, others had rags tied around their feet. Most soldiers had discarded their Army uniforms, while others wore them only in the darkness of night to keep warm. The daily struggle for survival, the unsuccessful searches for their loved ones, and the constant reminders of a lost war had robbed them of their once proud stance. Accosting people as they ran by in packs, children who had been taken from air-raided cities and relocated in designated safety zones had learned the rules of street survival.

Tired and discouraged, we boarded the Wurzburg-bound train. We stood by the window and viewed in silence what was once Nuremberg. We had heard that unrelenting bombing raids had obliterated the city, but we had never seen such total chaos before. For miles, as far as the eye could see, burned-out shells of homes stood only because the mountains of rubble did not permit them to fall and come to rest. Uninhabitable buildings stood with gaping holes in their sides exposing denuded rooms, and the jagged remnants of walls thrust their ragged edges toward the heavens, lamenting their fate. Streets were now winding footpaths through piles of debris. Throughout the remainder of our trip, through Wurzburg and onto our final destination, Frankfurt/Main, Erna and I realized that our Fuhrer had gotten his wish. In 1944, as the Allies encircled the borders of Germany, shortly before his self-inflicted death Adolf Hitler had shifted responsibility and blame for Germany's military collapse onto his people. At meetings, he raved at his district leaders and generals that his people had betrayed him. They were cowards, and they deserved defeat, humiliation, and even death at the hands of Germany's enemies. Now, his wish was reality. Germany lay in ruins, its people were destitute, and the once-feared Army had been annihilated. Germany's regions were divided, and its borders were guarded by four allied nations.

Frankfurt, in twilight, was an image of grotesqueness and it embodied the savagery of war. The stately, centuries old stone and brick houses lay reduced to rubble that flowed like lava out into the streets. Weather-beaten cardboard signs with crude, black letters pointed the way to avenues and streets. As the train stopped, we noted that the customary friendliness toward strangers we took for granted at home was not present here. We encountered several rebuffs and misdirections before we located our lodging.

Bombing of Nuremburg on the night of January 2, 1945, caused more than 3,000 fires. Whole areas stood in flames and half of the city pictured here was unapproachable because of leaking gases. Additional firefighters came from Regensburg and other surrounding cities to help fight the fires but the conflagration was not contained until January 10, 1945. Over 200 died in one shelter and the death toll in the rest of the city could not be accurately estimated.

Cities throughout Germany were destroyed beyond recognition.

Living conditions after 1943 and after the war.

CHAPTER THIRTY

ANOTHER WORLD — A LAND OF PEACE

Erna and I sensed that we had entered a different world while we criss-crossed through rows of American trucks, jeeps and cars. Suddenly, an American Military police officer stopped us. He carefully checked my passport and Erna's visiting permit. He called ahead, and motioned for us to enter the hotel.

As we entered a American interpreter met us and explained that Congressman Harold Hagen from Crookston, Minnesota, wanted assurance of my safe transfer to Frankfurt's Military Airport.

It was difficult for us to grasp the sudden transformation of citizens' rights. Instantly, we had privileges that a few hours ago would have been unattainable for anyone with a German ID. We had our own room with an unlimited supply of water, soap, and towels. Erna and I loved the fragrance of the big bar of *Lux* soap. Quickly, we tore the wrapper, we splashed water on each other, and caressed our faces with soapy foam until our cheeks turned rosy. We would have kept on with the soap and water play, but another surprise awaited us. Soldiers brought food.

Savoring the delectable aroma of the chicken dinner, I asked, "Erna, can you imagine anyone getting so much food for one meal?"

"Even Papa would have a hard time getting that much food on the black market, but he surely would try if he knew it could be had. Why, we don't get this much meat in three weeks!"

"Speaking of Papa," she continued in a whisper looking pensively at me, "what would you do? I am talking about Gerhard."

"Hey, don't blush, and you don't have to whisper." I turned my head and took in the whole room, "See, your papa isn't here."

"I am not like you, Anneliese, I can't stand up to him. I will marry Hans because Papa said I'd better."

"Your papa wants you to marry Hans because he is a landowner. He can't make you marry Hans. Just say no! You told me you love Gerhard, so marry him."

"Papa said that Gerhard is a refugee looking for a business."

"That's not true. Gerhard loves you and you're good for each other. If I were you, I would marry Gerhard. Since the church does not sanction divorce, what could your papa do, once you are married?"

Erna looked horrified. "You know Papa would go to the bishop and have the marriage annulled, and then he would surely disown me. He always tells me, 'You will have a good life, Erna, just do it my way.'" She dabbed her eyes with her handkerchief, and, composed, she continued. "Enough — nothing will ever change for me. Let's get some sleep." She turned from me. "Good night, Anneliese, sleep well during your last night in Germany. Tomorrow will be Easter."

I reached out to Erna, but she turned away and readied herself for bed. We laid near each other, we tossed and turned, but we remained silent. Even in the morning Erna didn't respond to my cheery "good morning," and she remained silent while I washed and dressed. I wondered if I had hurt her feelings, talking about Hans as I had.

Just then, someone walked back and forth on the other side of the door. "Miss Soooelk — Miss Sooooelk," he called out. Erna came quickly to my side and opened the door. Two American soldiers smiled at us and handed Erna and me a breakfast tray. We thanked them and inhaled the aroma of steaming hot food and coffee.

"Erna, just look at these scrambled eggs heaped high, toasted, buttered bread, and there is enough cream, sugar and honey to last for a week."

Erna looked at her tray. "Do you suppose in America you will get food like this everyday? For every meal?"

"They too use food stamps, but I think they do get more than we do," I said.

Our jovial mood was replaced by uncertainty as someone called my name. Slowly I opened the door and a soldier who called himself Texas informed us in fluent German, "I'll drive you to the airport, be ready in forty-five minutes. OK?"

When Texas returned he carried my wicker suitcase to his jeep and motioned for us to join him. He drove swiftly through the bombed out streets and navigated around piles of rubble with an assurance that we feared and admired. All too soon, the makeshift airport buildings, a high wire fence, and two American soldiers guarding the gate stood before us.

Texas stood quietly by while Erna and I held on to each other and exchanged our final good-byes and good wishes. "Anneliese, she said, "Take this and don't open it until you are on the plane."

"Erna, I don't think I can do it!" I cried out. "I know now, that I can't go in there and get on the plane!" I moved toward her, and resolutely I pushed her aside. "Erna, I am going back with you!" I shouted.

Erna blocked me, and commanded, "Anneliese, stop it! Stop it now! God forgive me for saying this, if you back out now, you'll always wonder and never be happy. You get on that plane, right now. Go, and you will be alright!"

She pushed me gently forward. "I think they are waiting for you, so go and remember to greet Kenny for me."

I nodded and without looking back I walked beside Texas to the gate. The guard carefully checked my official entry permit and in broken German phrases directed me to the airport waiting area.

Texas stopped, extended his hand, and smiled. "Greet America for me," he said. "Good-bye, and good luck."

Too late did I realized that I had entered a world of American personnel, and I listened intently because their words were as meaningless as their laughter. What had I done? Besides I love you, my knowledge of English was limited to a few words: Yes — no — hot — cold — and the town where Kenny lived, Crookston, Minnesota. My heart pounded, and I longed for Mama. 'If only she could be here and push me in the right direction.' I thought. Just as I wished that I could make myself inconspicuous, a tall American Military Police officer with a nightstick under his arm swaggered toward me.

He smiled and asked in fluent German, "Fraulein, are you leaving for America?"

"Yes," I replied, intimidated by his manner and uniform.

"Do you have any German money with you?" he asked.

"Yes," I stammered, "three hundred marks and some small coins for change."

He removed his white gloves and extended his cupped hands. 'You must turn the German paper money in to me. It is the law!"

Deliberately, he counted as I handed him the bills. "Keep the coins," he added, "they will make nice souvenirs for someone."

He reached into his pocket and retrieved a form. "When you land in New York, show this to the custom officials. You will get American dollars in exchange. Now don't you lose this form," he advised with fatherly concern in his voice.

He took my arm and led me to the boarding area. "Within ten minutes you should be called to board the plane, and when that happens, just go through the gate. Good luck, Fraulein, and have a good trip," he smiled and walked away.

The gate opened for boarding and within minutes our plane climbed to heights unknown to me. The sudden change from the destruction of the land below to the peaceful immensity of the horizon made me feel vulnerable and helpless. The stewardesses were serving food, and soon after lunch the steady humming of the propellers lulled me into a deep sleep. Hours later, a passenger shook me gently.

"Newfoundland — we land," he said as he gestured downward.

After refueling, the passenger next to me had tried to draw me into a conversation, but after several fruitless attempts we fell silent. My inability to make myself understood or read short captions scared me. "Should I have left Germany at all? Should I have given the Military Police officer my money?" I pondered.

Unashamedly I let the tears flow. Reaching for a handkerchief, I felt Erna's package in my coat pocket. I retrieved it, quickly tore off the paper, and under a layer of cotton, was Erna's gold necklace. Its heart-shaped pendant opened easily, and Erna's likeness smiled at me. I missed her and my family already, and I cried silently until sleep overtook me. I looked up with a start when the stewardess who took care of me throughout the flight touched my shoulder. She pointed at the window, and said, "America, welcome to America."

She stayed by my side and we watched as the shoreline of New York with patches of land reaching out to the ocean stretched out before us. Out of habit, I searched for damaged houses until I recalled that I had come to a land where there was peace.

CHAPTER THIRTY-ONE

ARRIVAL

After the plane landed, the stewardess collected my luggage, smiled and motioned for me to stay back until most of the passengers had left the plane. Finally, she said, "Come."

With my first steps on American soil, I looked for Kenny in a boisterous group waving and shouting, but Kenny was not among them. The stewardess stroked my arm, "OK?" she asked.

I nodded, and she led me into a hall filled with uniformed men stamping papers and looking through suitcases. Uncertainty gripped me as a custom official took my bags from the stewardess who smiled, waved, and left. While one officer inspected my bags, another scrutinized my exit-entrance permits and then pushed several forms toward me. "Sign," he ordered and waited.

I couldn't read the document, so I hesitated and looked around for help. "Sign," he repeated. Reluctantly I signed.

He looked at my signature and said, "No . . . no. . . no! In America you nix Anneliese." He reached for a blank paper, deep in thought while he paused — and finally, he printed with great flourish. A-N-N-E-L-E-E. His voice rose as he slowly sounded out each letter. "A-N-N-E-L-E-E."

Was he talking about my name? My heart pounded, and with all the courage I could master, I protested, "No, no, Anneliese."

The official sighed, and his manner became conciliatory, "No! Now, you in America — not Germany." He pointed at me and repeated "In America, you nix Anneliese." His long index finger almost touched my nose. "You are Annelee, understand?"

Did I understand? Not knowing what to do, I again looked at the officials nearby who somberly watched our exchange.

I shivered as I took the pen, and with a few strokes, Annelee, my American name came into existence. I understood: In America, Anneliese would be no more.

Before I had time to reflect on what had just happened, a German speaking custom official told me, "Fraulein, your fiancé, Kenneth Woodstrom, is waiting impatiently behind this door. All we need from you is the fifty dollar Immigration Entry Fee."

Finally, something would go my way. I handed the official my U.S. Money Exchange Form. "Another counterfeit!" he exclaimed. "Where did you get this?"

He listened quietly to my explanation why my three hundred marks were with the Military Police Officer at the Frankfurt Airport and I was here with the form. Several officials conferred briefly and paged Kenny. I waited anxiously until finally, Kenny rushed toward me.

"Anneliese, Anneliese! You are here!"

I threw myself into his open arms, and we hugged and kissed, and clung to each other. As he released me, he said, "Come, we leave."

"No, Kenny." I pointed at my counterfeit form. "Kenny, me no dollars."

He looked puzzled. The immigration official, who stood near me, lost his authoritative composure. He looked at Kenny. "Here is your bride," he said. "She is a foreigner, but like all women, she needs money."

Kenny, displeased with the official's explanation why I was penniless, paid the fee. 'What are you doing?' I wanted to ask, but I froze in fear as the official who had changed my name held me back and stepped between us.

"Mister Woodstrom, you must leave and return to the waiting room until we have processed all the forms. It will take a while longer because we don't classify 'Enemy Aliens' everyday, you know."

The big iron gate clanged shut behind Kenny and I felt afraid and frustrated. Why had they taken Kenny away from me? Silently the official glanced at me while he stamped page after page of official documents. Finally, he handed me a sheet.

"Sign American name, Annelee," he instructed.

I couldn't read what I signed, but I wanted to get away and be with Kenny.

He pointed toward the gate. Hurriedly, I gathered my baggage, rushed through the narrow, open space, and stepped into the outside world where Kenny was waiting. The tension of the past hours drained away, eighteen months of longing, yearning for Kenny rushed through me, and oblivious of everything, I flung myself into his outstretched arms and sobbed, "Kenny! Kenny!"

I felt weak, yet safe and happy as I pressed my head against his chest until my sobs subsided.

Kenny enveloped me in his arms, "Anneliese, my Anneliese," he whispered. He looked at me, caressed my face, kissed my tear-streaked cheeks and asked, "How are you, and how is Mama?"

"Good, Mama. All good," I replied.

"Taxi? Taxi, Mister?" The strange, abrupt voice of a taxi driver invaded our world. "Downtown, Mister?"

Without waiting for an answer, the cab driver jumped out of his cab, opened the trunk, placed my wicker suitcase in its cavity, and shut the trunk with a thump. He stepped up, opened the back door, and with a flowing motion of his free arm helped me into the back seat. All the while he chewed on a soggy stub of a cigar and talked in rapid-fire staccato to Kenny without missing a beat.

The driver eased into the heavy noontime traffic. He spewed out an avalanche of angry words at anyone who passed us, and he returned waves and signs to his fellow cabbies while he maneuvered his own vehicle through the network of streets. I felt overwhelmed by the constant changes. As New York's skyscrapers dwarfed us, I wondered if the occupants of the top floors of these towers had the clouds for neighbors. Out of habit, I kept looking for the bombed out sections, but mile after mile, buildings and bridges were intact. At times, the panorama of buildings seemed almost close enough to touch, yet seconds later, a kaleidoscopic view flashed by.

Kenny handed me a small velveteen box. "Anneliese," he said and motioned, "Open."

I opened the box slowly. Kenny took the gold band set off by a small, sparkling diamond, knelt on the floor of the cab and took my hands in his.

"Anneliese, I love you. Will you be my wife?" he asked.

I reached for him. "Yes, yes, Kenny. I love you."

He placed the ring on my finger and promised, "I will make you happy."

The driver whipped into the driveway and pulled up to a smooth stop in front of a hotel. The noises of the constant stop-and-go traffic, the foreign sounding voices of well-dressed people in the hotel lobby, and the whining ride in the elevator overwhelmed me. Mama was right about one thing. Until I learned the language, I'd have to depend on the man I loved, the only person I knew in America. My heart pounded and unanswered questions raced through my mind as I followed Kenny to his room. I thought: This is the first time that I am alone with Kenny the civilian, looking handsome in his gray, pin-striped suit. Now, what will happen? Will he take me in his arms, hold me and kiss me, take me to bed, or will he wait until we are married? My heart pounded wildly as Mama came to mind. Ever since I was old enough to understand, she had admonished, "Anneliese, never give yourself to a man. You must be married before you sleep with him. You understand?"

We entered the room, and Kenny closed the door quietly behind us. He took me in his arms and we kissed passionately when suddenly, awkwardly, yet gently he pushed me away from him.

"You rest and freshen up?" He motioned toward the bathroom.

I wanted to stay in his arms, yet I was relieved when he didn't push me to make a decision just now. I felt reassured and secure because Kenny understood my needs for patience and time while I absorbed all the sudden changes that leaving Germany had thrust upon me. Feeling secure, I slept soundly until Kenny woke me and asked, "Hungry? We go eat?"

The hotel dining room was a new world for me. There was so much to see, so much to learn. I looked at a menu I couldn't read, listened intently to conversations I couldn't understand, and I watched with fascination as the waiter balanced a tray laden with food and drink.

"All mine?" I asked. The plate before me was heaped with a chicken dinner, and throughout the meal I looked on in wonder as.the waiter, without being asked, frequently checked the basket of hard rolls, filled our cups with coffee and carried leftovers away. I wondered if Kenny has used all his ration stamps for this one meal.

All too soon I found that my shrunken stomach tolerated only small amounts of food. Since 1943 our daily food rations consisted of fifty grams, or approximately two ounces of meat, two ounces of coffee grounds, two ounces of shortening, and two ounces of sugar for each person. The weekly rations were two pounds of bread, four pounds of potatoes, and two cups of skim milk --- if it was available.

I always ate every crumb on my plate, yet the only time I felt full was during the night when in my dreams banquets fit for the Fuhrer would magically appear, and I could eat all my favorite food until hunger pains and thirst awakened me.

My heart ached as I looked around the dining room and saw all the good food left behind. My family could feast for at least a week and hunger would not be their steady companion.

Kenny led me outside and we boarded a bus to the shopping district of New York. I stared in disbelief at the displays set up in windows and outdoor showcases overflowed with merchandise. At home, I thought, these cases would be emptied within minutes by starving hordes of people while here, no one even waited in line. There were cars, buses, and people, there was order and everyone knew where they were going.

We stopped at Gimbles, where Kenny led me through the aisles. I felt I had entered Heaven's Christmas Land. I wanted to look, touch, and look again before everything disappeared. Kenny held my hand tightly as we stepped on the moving wonder, the escalator took us safely to the shoe department on the fourth floor.

A salesman looked at my worn-out shoes and asked, "Europe?"

"Yes," replied Kenny. "She needs shoes."

The salesman thoroughly enjoyed fitting me with a new pair of high-heeled, black patent leather shoes. They fit so well and they were more beautiful than any shoes that I, or anyone else in my family, had ever owned.

"Herr Mayor," I said to myself, "you were right! I could get a pair of shoes in America. 'Just like that!'"

I couldn't stop looking at my new shoes as Kenny took me to women's clothing. There were no tailors, yet we passed endless rows of coats, suits, dresses, skirts, and blouses. Kenny spoke with someone, and within minutes two saleswomen took me in hand and eagerly replaced everything I wore. My thoughts drifted home where yearly applications for new clothing had resulted in denial slips and yet another application to the mayor's office. Alone in the dressing room, I caressed my new underwear, the sheer nylons, the variegated wool suit with matching accessories, and of course, my new shoes. How could all this be for me? I turned on my new shoes, and I could see my reflection in the black patent leather. I felt like Cinderella going to the ball, and again and again, I looked and touched, tucked here and there, while "Annelee" smiled at me. My heart burst with joy as the saleswomen brought a new coat, a matching hat, purse and gloves, but I shook my head resolutely, "No!" The new coat was beautiful, but I needed to keep my own black coat, the only "new" apparel I had brought from home.

Kenny, who had been waiting patiently, whistled softly as he saw me approach. Somehow I felt transformed as we left Gimbles. I realized that surely, no one could tell by looking at me, that I was an Enemy Alien from Germany.

"Mama, you will see," I whispered, "if I don't leave Kenny's side, I will be fine, and everything will be all right."

As if to prove my point, Kenny hailed a taxi to Grand Central Station. Momentary flashes of the depot in Nuremberg, the chaos and despair I had seen and experienced a few days ago, overtook me. As we settled ourselves in our compartment I felt tired, and within minutes the train's click-clack mesmerized me into a fitful sleep.

Kenny shook me gently. "Anneliese, wake up. Washington D.C.," he said softly.

He busied himself with our baggage while I listened to the hustle and bustle of the passengers around us. It was dusk outside, and I watched as the sun nested down between buildings on the western horizon. Somewhere, out there, Kenny's parents were waiting to meet me.

As we left Union Station, a taxi driver called out to us and then he extended his hand to me.

"Welcome to America, Fraulein," he said.

Kenny motioned and said, "Friend, we stay at his house."

The driver joined the evening traffic. The darkness of the night did not penetrate the streets of Washington, D.C. Lights glared everywhere, yet the traffic flowed smoothly and steadily. I found no chaos here, nor morbid darkness. Everything was so unlike the Germany I had known these past eight years.

I continued deep in thought while Kenny and the driver talked. Suddenly, Kenny put his hands over my eyes and made sure I could not peek out. I was in complete darkness. My heart pounded and my thoughts raced. "What is it, Kenny? What can't I see? Ah, I have it, your ghettos and the night people. That's it, isn't it? Were we approaching those places I had read about at home?"

I moved restlessly, and Kenny laughed. "Anneliese, you will see."

The taxi stopped. Kenny removed his hands. Lights engulfed everything around us, and the brightness made me blink rapidly. Abruptly, I sucked in my breath and shivered as goose bumps crawled through my skin. Wonderstruck, I sat quietly. The beauty and the massiveness of the Capitol Building was beyond anything I could have imagined. It seemed the past and the future had merged right here and penetrated into the very interior of our car. Thoughts and feelings bombarded and captivated my whole being. I felt so small and insignificant, yet so special at the same time. I hugged my own body and sat still until Kenny spoke to the driver. He started the car and we were silent while he drove past the White House, the house where President Harry Truman lived. Slowly, I understood that I was truly in another world. How beautiful it was! How stately! How serene!

Realization crept into my mind and took hold. "So that is the way people live where there is peace!" I said softly. Tears welled up in my eyes until the lights were a blur. "If only Mama and everyone, everyone in the world could live where there is peace!"

I suddenly felt drained and sad. I had not known peace and serenity since I was in seventh grade waiting to celebrate my thirteenth birthday.

CHAPTER THIRTY-TWO

RED TAPE BEFORE MARRIAGE

Washington, D.C.

Kenny's friend drove on slowly, and the magic of the moment faded as apprehension gripped me. Soon I would stand face to face with Kenny's parents who had traveled with Kenny from Crookston, Minnesota, to meet me. All too soon we turned in to a long curved driveway and stopped in front of an English Tudor home owned by Kenny's friend. My heart pounded in trip-hammer blows, and I didn't want to leave the safety of just Kenny and me.

"Welcome," the driver said, "I hope you will feel at home with us."

The massive front door opened from within, and we stepped into the foyer. Straight ahead, a large crystal chandelier hung from the ceiling, its glistening crystals and the antique dining room furniture added old-world elegance. Kenny left our baggage near the curved stairway, and we walked hand in hand up to the second floor where Kenny's father and Caroline, his mother, rushed toward us.
"Welcome to our family," they said sincerely. They shook my hand and asked, "Anneliese, how are you?"

"Good, good," I replied.

They led us to their suite, and they eagerly questioned Kenny while I sat listening, without understanding. As the clock struck midnight, it became hard for me to keep focus, and the voices around me faded while I yawned and struggled to stay awake. Kenny was instantly by my side and took me in his arms while he spoke to his mother.

"Anneliese," she said, cupping her hands by her cheek and motioning, "Sleep?"

Gently, she led me to an adjoining bedroom, turned the covers down, and stayed by my side until I crawled into bed. In Germany it was 6:00 a.m., dawn was breaking, and the sun was rising. Loneliness welled up within me and I tried to suppress the tears that flowed down my checks while I wished for Mama at my side. Kenny's mother stroked my hair and my shoulders while she talked softly in words I couldn't understand, but her presence soothed my pain and my sobbing waned.

"Better?" she asked.

I nodded and pulled the covers tightly around me. She got up, turned on a small light, and whispered, "Good night," as she closed the door quietly.

The strangeness of my surroundings kept me awake. What had I done? I couldn't understand anyone who spoke to me, not even Kenny. I felt like a child...a two year old was more understood than I was. The only English words I knew were "Hot," "Cold," "Crookston, Minnesota," "I love you," "Yes" and "No." If someone asked me a question, I could only guess at whether it should be answered with "Yes" or "No."

Why hadn't I listened to Mama? Why did I leave home? Why did Erna block my way from going back home? I would have left the Frankfurt Airport with her, and I would be home in my own bed. Better yet, I should have asked Kenny to live in Germany with me. My thoughts raced on. Maybe Kenny's parents would find that they did not like me and send me home. In my imagination, Uncle Pepp laughed, "Ah, ha, you couldn't take it for two years? I knew you would come home!"

"Never, never!" I uttered. Feeling better, I drifted off to sleep.

I awoke to life-changing events that crowded the day. After breakfast, Kenny showed me his shiny, black 1936 Ford, and he said proudly, "Ours, yours and mine. Come, we must meet with Congressman Hagen."

We joined the moving sea of cars and Kenny maneuvered our vehicle along an interwoven band of highways until, as suddenly as the night before, the Capitol building loomed ahead. We merged with people, and huge elevators lifted us to Congressman Hagen's office. Kenny was well acquainted with the secretaries and everyone was aware of my arrival.

A young woman spoke to me in broken German. Pointing at

several people, she explained, "We worked on your papers so you might come to America."

A tall, gray-haired man approached us and Kenny introduced him, "The Honorable Congressman Harold Hagen." Turning toward me, he said, "Anneliese."

Congressman Hagen extended both hands to Kenny and me while a young woman stood beside him and translated.

"Welcome to America, Anneliese, we do hope you will like it here. Let us hope there is no more red tape left to untangle, and we can get you and Kenny married without further delay."

He brought Kenny up-to-date on our scheduled appointments and they talked of tomorrow, our wedding day. Finally, eighteen months of hard work came to conclusion. During January 1947, Kenny had taken a leave from his work, so he could be in Washington, and come to the Congressional Office whenever they needed him.

At the same time, I had tried to do my part in Germany. Barefooted, I had walked ten miles during October, November, and December 1945, and every week, I came home empty-handed, without a letter. When the mail service improved, I hitchhiked, walked, and rode on freight trains to the American Consulate in Munich. No one believed that I, a German Enemy Alien, could have a chance of ever accomplishing what Kenny and I had set out to do. Yet, tomorrow, we would be married.

The next morning Congressman Hagen's personal secretary, Mister Child, accompanied us to Arlington, Virginia, and would act as my interpreter. As we entered the court house, he cautioned, "Kenny, since you will marry an Enemy Alien, it may take several hours before all the documents are ready for our signatures."

The court house office was old and small. On one side of the wall was a long, wooden bench where I sat and waited while the men filled out forms. The clerk climbed a ladder, reached for a book and read specific passages while Kenny and Mister Child listened.

I wondered, "Is all this necessary to fill out a marriage license?"

Finally, they approached me, pointing at the discrepancies of my name.

"Exit Permit Anneliese Solch and Entry Permit 'Annelee

Solch'?" the clerk asked.

I felt relieved.   I explained and Mr. Child translated, "Anneliese in Germany, always. In America, the immigration officer told me I must always write Annelee."

The men conferred with each other, and they were satisfied with my explanation of how Annelee came into existence.   The clerk's second question was more difficult for me to comprehend. He showed me the official German document, in which Mama had given me permission to come to the United States and marry Kenny.

"You are not twenty-one until September," the clerk said. He pointed at the blank line below Mama's signature, "I need your father's signature, right here."

I shook my head and stated, "Papa in Russia."

Kenny explained that Papa was a prisoner of war in Russia and we had not heard from him since 1945. The clerk shook his head and motioned for the men to follow him. Mister Child was talking with someone on the phone while Kenny and the clerk were bent over several books.   They conferred for sometime and then Kenny motioned as he said, "Anneliese, come, back to Washington."

I wondered silently if our religious differences would create another problem before the clerk would issue our marriage license. It was early afternoon when Congressman Hagen assured us that we could get married since a rider to the Enemy Alien Marriage Amendment accepting either parent's permission had been passed. Finally, at eight o'clock as darkness engulfed Washington, the clerk of court issued our marriage license.   The Catholic priest, the Lutheran minister, and the Justice of Peace who had been asked to stand by had long since left.   But Congressman Hagen had stayed in his office until he found a Presbyterian minister who agreed to marry a Roman Catholic who was an Enemy Alien and an Evangelical Lutheran in his home. Everyone's efforts capsulized and within the hour we would be married.

Kenny found the address where we were all to meet and we were ushered into the living room where the minister was waiting. I was not familiar with the brief passage he read from the Bible, and without understanding I repeated the foreign words of the marriage vows. The minister shook my hand, and Kenny kissed me gently and held me tight. My in-laws embraced us and gave their blessings.

Everyone returned with us to Mister Child's home where the secretaries and personnel celebrated the finalization of eighteen months of working for this day. They were happy for us, and they showered us with gifts and good wishes While their genuine caring overwhelmed me, their presence fueled the longing for my family. They should have been here with me. I missed their hugs and good wishes.

I wanted for my heart to be still and not reveal my sudden loneliness. It was my wedding day, the day I had longed and waited for, and I was supposed to be happy. I was — but I knew I was not the "glowing with happiness" bride.

Kenny looked at me and came to my side, "We must leave," he said. "It has been a long and special day for Anneliese and me. We are happy, but I also know that my wife must be exhausted."

Mr. Child said in German, "Anneliese, we are so glad we finally met and we are happy for you and Kenny. When you are fluent in English, we hope you share with Congressman Hagen and us what it was like to live in Adolf Hitler's Germany."

Kenny assured them that I would. While Kenny drove, he reached quietly for my hand and clasped his fingers tightly around mine. Happiness, exhaustion, and homesickness all these emotions made me weepy. We had reached the English Tudor home where we were staying. At the top of the stairs, Kenny's parents came up to me, hugged me and said, "Good Night, and God Bless."

We entered our room, we embraced and our kisses brought fulfillment as we belonged to each other. Now we were truly husband and wife. All the changes of the past days and hours kept me wide awake. It was morning in Germany and I wondered how my family coped with my absence. I thought about the interpreter's request and wondered.

These kind people in America wanted to hear about Adolf Hitler, the man who is despised everywhere in the world. How could I tell them that as a child, during 1935, I wanted nothing more than to be a member of Adolf Hitler's Jung Maidens' organization? Would they understand or would they hold it against me? I had no answer. Time would tell if my new family and the people around me could understand the frightening power of indoctrination.

Our Wedding Picture
April 1947

50 Years Later

To order additional copies of
WAR CHILD - Growing Up In Adolf Hitler's Germany
please complete the following.

$16.95 EACH
(plus $3.95 shipping & handling for first book,
add $2.00 for each additional book ordered.

Shipping and Handling costs for larger quantites
available upon request.

Please send me _____ additional books at $16.95 + shipping & handling

Bill my: ❏ VISA   ❏ MasterCard   Expires _____

Card # _____

Signature _____

Daytime Phone Number _____

For credit card orders call 1-888-568-6329
TO ORDER ON-LINE VISIT: www.jmcompanies.com
OR SEND THIS ORDER FORM TO:
McCleery & Sons Publishing
PO Box 248
Gwinner, ND 58040-0248

I am enclosing $_____   ❏ Check ❏ Money Order
Payable in US funds. No cash accepted.

SHIP TO:
Name _____

Mailing Address _____

City _____

State/Zip _____

Orders by check allow longer delivery time.
Money order and credit card orders will be shipped within 48 hours.
This offer is subject to change without notice.

NEW RELEASES

The SOE on Enemy Soil
Churchill's Elite Force
British Prime Minister Winston Churchill's plan for liberating Europe from the Nazis during the darkest days of the Second World War was ambitious: provide a few men and women, most of them barely out of their teens, with training in subversion and hand-to-hand combat, load them down with the latest in sophisticated explosives, drop them by parachute into the occupied countries, then sit back and wait for them to "Set Europe Ablaze." No story been told with more honesty and humor than Sergeant Fallick tells his tale of service. The training, the fear, the tragic failures, the clandestine romances, and the soldiers' high jinks are all here, warmly told from the point of view of "one bloke" who experienced it all and lived to tell about it.
Written by R.A. Fallick. (282 pgs.)
$16.95 each in a 6x9" paperback.

Blue Darkness
This tale of warm relationships and chilling murders takes place in the lake country of central Minnesota. Normal activities in the small town of New Dresen are disrupted when local resident, ex-CIA agent Maynard Cushing, is murdered. His killer, Robert Ranforth also an ex-CIA agent, had been living anonymously in the community for several years. Earlier in his career, Cushing was instrumental during the investigation and subsequent arrest of Ranforth by the FBI for espionage. Ranforth vanished before the trial began. Tom Hastings, a neighbor and friend of the victim, becomes a threat to the anonymous ex-agent. Stalked and attached at his country home, he employs tools and people, including neighbors, a deputy sheriff and Allan Burnside of the FBI, to mount a defense and help solve crimes.
Written by Ernest Francis Schanilec. (276 pgs.)
$16.95 each in a 6x9" paperback.

War Child
Growing Up in Adolf Hitler's Germany
Annelee Woodstrom was twenty years old when she immigrated to America in 1947. These kind people in America wanted to hear about Adolf Hitler, the man who was despised everywhere in the world. During her adolescene, constant propaganda and strictly enforced censorship influenced her thinking. As a young adult, the bombings and all the consequential suffering caused by World War II affected Annelee deeply. How could Annelee tell them that as a child, during 1935, she wanted nothing more than to be a member of Adolf Hitler's Jung Maidens' organization? Written by Annelee Woodstrom (252 pgs.)
$16.95 each in a 6x9" paperback.

Grandmother Alice
Memoirs from the Home Front Before Civil War into 1930's
Alice Crain Hawkins could be called the 'Grandma Moses of Literature'. Her stories, published for the first time, were written while an invalid during the last years of her life. These journal entries from the late 1920's and early 30's gives us a fresh, novel and unique understanding of the lives of those who lived in the upper part of South Carolina during the state's growing years. Alice and her ancestors experiences are filled with understanding - they are provacative and profound. Written by Reese Hawkins (178 pgs.) $16.95 each in a 6x9" paperback.

I Took The Easy Way Out
Life Lessons on Hidden Handicaps
Twenty-five years ago, Tom Day was managing a growing business - holding his own on the golf course and tennis court. He was living in the fast lane. For the past 25 years, Tom has spent his days in a wheelchair with a spinal cord injury. Attendants serve his every need. What happened to Tom? We get an honest account of the choices Tom made in his life. It's a courageous story of reckoning, redemption and peace. Written by Thomas J. Day. (200 pgs.) $19.95 each in a 6x9" paperback.

Tales & Memories of Western North Dakota
Prairie Tales & True Stories of 20th Century Rural Life
This manuscript has been inspired with Steve's antidotes, bits of wisdom and jokes (sometimes ethnic, to reflect the melting pot that was and is North Dakota; and from most unknown sources). A story about how to live life with humor, courage and grace along with personal hardships, tragedies and triumphs. Written by Steve Taylor. (174 pgs.) $14.95 each in a 6x9" paperback.

9/11 and Meditation - *America's Handbook*
All Americans have been deeply affected by the terrorist events of and following 9-11-01 in our country. David Thorson submits that meditation is a potentially powerful intervention to ameliorate the frightening effects of such divisive and devastating acts of terror. This book features a lifetime of harrowing life events amidst intense pychological and social polarization, calamity and chaos; overcome in part by practicing the age-old art of meditation. Written by David Thorson. (110 pgs.) $9.95 each in a 4-1/8 x 7-1/4" paperback.

Eat, Drink & Remarry
The poetry in this book is taken from different experiences in Lynne's life and from different geographical and different emotional places.
Every poem is an inspiration from someone or a direct event from their life...or from hers. Every victory and every mistake - young or old. They slowly shape and mold you into the unique person you are. Celebrate them as rough times that you were strong enough to endure. By sharing them with others, there will always be one person who will learn from them. Written by Lynne D. Richard Larson (86 pgs.)
$12.95 each in a 5x8" paperback.

Phil Lempert's HEALTHY, WEALTHY, & WISE
The Shoppers Guide for Today's Supermarket
This is the must-have tool for getting the most for your money in every aisle. With this valuable advice you will never see (or shop) the supermarket the same way again. You will learn how to: save at least $1,000 a year on your groceries, guarantee satisfaction on every shopping trip, get the most out of coupons or rebates, avoid marketing gimmicks, create the ultimate shopping list, read and understand the new food labels, choose the best supermarkets for you and your family. Written by Phil Lempert. (198 pgs.)
$9.95 each in a 6x9" paperback.

Miracles of COURAGE
The Larry W. Marsh Story
This story is for anyone looking for simple formulas for overcoming insurmountable obstacles. At age 18, Larry lost both legs in a traffic accident and learned to walk again on untested prothesis. No obstacle was too big for him - putting himself through college - to teaching a group of children that frustrated the whole educational system - to developing a nationally recognized educational program to help these children succeed. Written by Linda Marsh. (134 pgs.)
$12.95 each in a 6x9" paperback.

The Garlic Cure
Learn about natural breakthroughs to outwit: Allergies, Arthritis, Cancer, Candida Albicans, Colds, Flu and Sore Throat, Environmental and Body Toxins, Fatigue, High Cholesterol, High Blood Pressure and Homocysteine and Sinus Headaches. The most comprehensive, factual and brightly written health book on garlic of all times. INCLUDES: 139 GOURMET GARLIC RECIPES! Written by James F. Scheer, Lynn Allison and Charlie Fox. (240 pgs.)
$14.95 each in a 6x9" paperback.

For Your Love
Janelle, a spoiled socialite, has beauty and breeding to attract any mate she desires. She falls for Jared, an accomplished man who has had many lovers, but no real love. Their hesitant romance follows Jared and Janelle across the ocean to exciting and wild locations. Join in a romance and adventure set in the mid-1800's in America's grand and proud Southland.
Written by Gunta Stegura. (358 pgs.)
$16.95 each in a 6x9" paperback.

From Graystone to Tombstone
Memories of My Father Engolf Snortland 1908-1976
This haunting memoir will keep you riveted with true accounts of a brutal penitentiary to a manhunt in the unlikely little town of Tolna, North Dakota. At the same time the reader will emerge from the book with a towering respect for the author, a man who endured pain, grief and needless guilt -- but who learned the art of forgiving and writes in the spirit of hope. Written by Roger Snortland. (178 pgs.)
$16.95 each in a 6x9" paperback.

Blessed Are The Peacemakers
Civil War in the Ozarks
A rousing tale that traces the heroic Rit Gatlin from his enlistment in the Confederate Army in Little Rock to his tragic loss of a leg in a Kentucky battle, to his return in the Ozarks. He becomes engaged in guerilla warfare with raiders who follow no flag but their own. Rit finds himself involved with a Cherokee warrior, slaves and romance in a land ravaged by war.
Written by Joe W. Smith (444 pgs.)
$19.95 each in a 6 x 9 paperback

Pycnogenol®
Pycnogenol® for Superior Health presents exciting new evidence about nature's most powerful antioxidant. Pycnogenol® improves your total health, reduces risk of many diseases, safeguards your arteries, veins and entire circulation system. It protects your skin - giving it a healthier, smoother younger glow. Pycnogenol® also boosts your immune system. Read about it's many other beneficial effects. Written by Richard A. Passwater, Ph.D. (122 pgs.)
$5.95 each in a 4-1/8 x 6-7/8" paperback.

Remembering Louis L'Amour
Reese Hawkins was a close friend of Louis L'Amour, one of the fastest selling writers of all time. Now Hawkins shares this friendship with L'Amour's legion of fans. Sit with Reese in L'Amour's study where characters were born and stories came to life. Travel with Louis and Reese in the 16 photo pages in this memoir. Learn about L'Amour's lifelong quest for knowledge and his philosophy of life. Written by Reese Hawkins and his daughter Meredith Hawkins Wallin. (178 pgs.)
$16.95 each in a 5-1/2x8" paperback.

Outward Anxiety - Inner Calm
Steve Crociata is known to many as the Optician to the Stars. He was diagnosed with a baffling form of cancer. The author has processed experiences in ways which uniquely benefit today's readers. We learn valuable lessons on how to cope with distress, how to marvel at God, and how to win at the game of life.
Written by Steve Crociata (334 pgs.)
$19.95 each in a 6 x 9 paperback

Seasons With Our Lord
Original seasonal and special event poems written from the heart. Feel the mood with the tranquil color photos facing each poem. A great coffee table book or gift idea. Written by Cheryl Lebahn Hegvik. (68 pgs.) $24.95 each in a 11x8-1/2 paperback.

Bonanza Belle

In 1908, Carrie Amundson left her home to become employed on a bonanza farm. Carrie married and moved to town. One tragedy after the other befell her and altered her life considerably and she found herself back on the farm where her family lived the toiled during the Great Depression. Carrie was witness to many life-changing events happenings. She changed from a carefree girl to a woman of great depth and stamina.
Written by Elaine Ulness Swenson. (344 pgs.)
$15.95 each in a 6x8-1/4" paperback.

Home Front

Read the continuing story of Carrie Amundson, whose life in North Dakota began in *Bonanza Belle*. This is the story of her family, faced with the challenges, sacrifices and hardships of World War II. Everything changed after the Pearl Harbor attack, and ordinary folk all across America, on the home front, pitched in to help in the war effort. Even years after the war's end, the effects of it are still evident in many of the men and women who were called to serve their country. Written by Elaine Ulness Swenson. (304 pgs.)
$15.95 each in a 6x8-1/4" paperback.

First The Dream

This story spans ninety years of Anna's life - from Norway to America - to finding love and losing love. She and her family experience two world wars, flu epidemics, the Great Depression, droughts and other quirks of Mother Nature and the Vietnam War. A secret that Anna has kept is fully revealed at the end of her life.
Written by Elaine Ulness Swenson. (326 pgs.)
$15.95 each in a 6x8-1/4" paperback

Pay Dirt

An absorbing story reveals how a man with the courage to follow his dream found both gold and unexpected adventure and adversity in Interior Alaska, while learning that human nature can be the most unpredictable of all.
Written by Otis Hahn & Alice Vollmar. (168 pgs.)
$15.95 each in a 6x9" paperback.

Spirits of Canyon Creek
Sequel to "Pay Dirt"

Hahn has a rich stash of true stories about his gold mining experiences. This is a continued successful collaboration of battles on floodwaters, facing bears and the discovery of gold in the Yukon.
Written by Otis Hahn & Alice Vollmar. (138 pgs.)
$15.95 each in a 6x9" paperback.

Whispers in the Darkness

In this fast paced, well thought out mystery with a twist of romance, Betty Pearson comes to a slow paced, small town. Little did she know she was following a missing link - what the dilapidated former Beardsley Manor she was drawn to, held for her. With twists and turns, the Manor's secrets are unraveled. Written by Shirlee Taylor. (88 pgs.)
$14.95 each in a 6x9" paperback.

Dr. Val Farmer's Honey, I Shrunk The Farm

The first volume in a three part series of Rural Stress Survival Guides discusses the following in seven chapters: Farm Economics; Understanding The Farm Crisis; How To Cope With Hard Times; Families Going Through It Together; Dealing With Debt; Going For Help, Helping Others and Transitions Out of Farming. Written by Val Farmer. (208 pgs.)
$16.95 each in a 6x9" paperback.

Country-fied

Stories with a sense of humor and love for country and small town people who, like the author, grew up country-fied . . . Country-fied people grow up with a unique awareness of their dependence on the land. They live their lives with dignity, hard work, determination and the ability to laugh at themselves. Written by Elaine Babcock. (184 pgs.)
$14.95 each in a 6x9" paperback.

Charlie's Gold and Other Frontier Tales

Kamron's first collection of short stories gives you adventure tales about men and women of the west, made up of cowboys, Indians, and settlers. Written by Kent Kamron. (174 pgs.) $15.95 each in a 6x9" paperback.

A Time For Justice

This second collection of Kamron's short stories takes off where the first volume left off, satisfying the reader's hunger for more tales of the wide prairie. Written by Kent Kamron. (182 pgs.) $16.95 each in a 6x9" paperback.

It Really Happened Here!

Relive the days of farm-to-farm salesmen and hucksters, of ghost ships and locust plagues when you read Ethelyn Pearson's collection of strange but true tales. It captures the spirit of our ancestors in short, easy to read, colorful accounts that will have you yearning for more. Written by Ethelyn Pearson. (168 pgs.) $24.95 each in an 8-1/2x11" paperback.

(Add $3.95 shipping & handling for first book, add $2.00 for each additional book ordered.)